PUPPETS, POEMS,& SONGS

BY JULIE CATHERINE SHELTON

FEARON TEACHER AIDS

A Paramount Communications Company

To my family—

Because I love you and you've waited a long time for this.

Editorial Director: Virginia L. Murphy
Editor: Carol Williams
Copyeditors: Lisa Schwimmer and Kristin Eclov
Cover and Inside Illustration: Janet Skiles
Cover Design: Lucyna Green
Design: Diann Abbott
Production: Rebecca Speakes

ISBN 0-8224-5152-2

Printed in the United States of America
1. 9 8 7 6 5 4 3 2 1

CONTENTS

CONTENTS

CONTENTS

CONTENTS

INTRODUCTION

Children love poems and songs and they have a natural attraction to the feel and sound of the spoken language. They delight in rhyme, repetition, and alliteration long before they fully understand what the words actually mean. Even the very youngest children respond readily to the familiar rhythm and rhyme of "Pat-a-Cake" or "Itsy Bitsy Spider." Learning poems and songs is a great way for children to learn new vocabulary. Songs and poems are veritable treasures, filled with those very aspects of our language that children respond to most readily and unreservedly, and with the most emotional involvement.

Children also respond to puppets with tremendous enthusiasm. Yet, most puppet shows are much too long and complicated for the interest levels and attention spans of preschool and early elementary children. Not so with the presentations in this book. Each puppet is carefully designed to appeal to a small child's sense of wonder and delight.

The combination of puppets with poems and songs makes this book invaluable to early-childhood educators. Each theatrical presentation has successfully delighted children over and over again. Each chapter features the complete text for theme-related poems and songs that can be reproduced and mounted on 5" x 7" (12.7 cm x 17.7 cm) file cards for handy storage and use. With the poems and songs are patterns and instructions for making the puppets. Enlist the help of adult volunteers or older students in making the puppets. Or, invite the children to help create the puppets. The stage for each presentation is a box resting on your lap, which not only displays the puppets, but houses them for storage as well. Each chapter ends with a list of children's books that you can use to enhance your thematic unit.

The poems and songs in each chapter are arranged in recommended order of presentation. Present the poems

INTRODUCTION

and songs in each chapter all together as a curriculum-enhancing unit. Or, use individual poems and songs separately as attention-getters, signals for quiet-time activities, time fillers, rainy-day treats, or just plain fun. After presenting the poems and songs, you may want to place the materials in a learning center. Invite the children to reenact the poems and songs you presented or encourage the children to create their own puppet shows and present them to one another.

When you use the materials in this book, you will be educating, entertaining, and enriching children by:

- enlarging the scope of their world,
- developing their group interaction skills,
- encouraging active use of their imaginations,
- improving their listening and pre-reading skills,
- enhancing their appreciation of art and music,
- laying a solid foundation for their language-arts skills, and
- fostering a love of books and reading that will last a lifetime.

Puppets, Poems, & Songs will provide you and the children with many years of enjoyment and satisfaction.

MATERIALS & SUPPLIES

.All of the puppets described in this book can be made from inexpensive, readily obtained materials. However, since there are so many different types of materials available, here are some recommendations, helpful hints, and ideas for substitutions.

BAMBOO SKEWERS

These are $1/8$" x 12" (3 mm x 30.5 cm) round bamboo sticks used for barbecuing. They have sharp, pointed ends that are perfect for inserting into other materials to use as puppet manipulators or to hold the puppets during the presentations. They can also be used in place of drinking straws for stick puppets. Skewers can be found in the housewares section of most large department stores, specialty kitchen shops, and stores that sell gas grills and other barbecuing equipment.

CHRISTMAS ORNAMENTS

Many Christmas ornaments are actually miniatures that can be used as puppets. In the past few years, I have purchased cornhusk mice, stuffed lamé stars, elves, knitted mittens, hats and socks, painted wooden Mother Goose figures, sleds, teddy bears, fuzzy sheep, muslin geese, wrapped presents, clowns, strings of plastic candy and popcorn, wooden trains, dolls, cloth people, apples, musical instruments, all sorts of feathered birds, baskets, and nosegays, just to name a few. The list is endless. Shop in stores that specialize exclusively in Christmas merchandise and you'll be amazed by what you may find.

CRAYONS

Any brand of wax crayons will do, but give yourself the broadest color range possible. Start with a box of 64 colors and replace the basic colors you use the most by buying additional boxes of 8, 16, or 24 colors.

EYES

Wiggly Eyes

These look like little plastic cases with a white backing, a clear cover, and a black ball or disk which moves around freely inside. These eyes range in size from 3 mm to 40 mm. Most are round, but there are some available in oval shapes. There are also assorted sizes available in pink, blue, green and yellow.

Crystal Eyes

These are half-rounded buttons with a stem. They come in a variety of sizes and colors with a round black pupil. These are excellent for animal puppets.

Cat Eyes

These are similar to crystal eyes, except the pupil is elongated rather than round. They are available in blue, yellow, orange, and green.

MATERIALS & SUPPLIES

Owl Eyes

These may be hard to find in smaller craft stores. An acceptable substitute is wiggly eyes of the same size.

Button Eyes

These are regular buttons that are either flat or half-round.

Half-Rounds

These come in two basic sizes—3 mm and 6 mm. They are little black plastic balls cut in half. These may not be available in every craft store, but if half-rounds are recommended and cannot be found, substitute round black beads or wiggly eyes of the same size.

FANCY TRIMS
Feathers

Feathers come in plastic bags that are usually sorted by color and type. The most common types are flats, plumage, marabou shorts, and marabou longs. Marabou shorts are the most useful. They can be obtained at most craft stores. Use them as hair, fringe, a delicate feature of flower faces, or wings on pom-pom birds. Feathers add a wonderful look and texture to puppets.

Sequins and Beads

These come in all sizes, shapes, and colors. Use red sequins as lights on a spaceship, round wheel beads as knobs on the ends of a butterfly's antennae, or other shapes as earrings and costume decorations.

Chenille Stems

These are pipe cleaners that are a bit longer and a little fatter than ordinary pipe cleaners. They also come in a wide variety of colors as well as silver, gold, and other shiny metallics.

Bumpy Chenille

These are chenille stems with bumps at regular intervals. You can get regular bumpy chenille and jumbo bumpy chenille (which has fatter bumps that are farther apart).

Curly Chenille

Curly chenille comes in several colors and is great for puppet hair. In the package, curly chenille looks like long, shiny worms or fat spaghetti. Curly chenille is long, flexible tubes of fibers held together by connecting threads running up through the centers. Each piece is $1/4$ inch (6 mm) in diameter and looks like thin, shiny ringlets. Curly chenille can be cut, shaped, and glued with ease.

Loopy Chenille

Loopy chenille is available in a wide variety of colors and is great for puppet hair. These are about 1 inch (2.5 cm) wide and look like back-and-forth loops of acrylic yarn gathered down the middle by a central thread or wire. If you can't find loopy chenille in craft stores, try yarn and needlework shops or doll supply stores.

Felt

Felt is one of the most common materials needed to make the puppet projects. It will be less expensive in the long run if you buy a half yard of every color you can find. If possible, buy felt from the bolt, because it is often thicker and more substantial than craft squares. The dimensions given on each project page are approximate and are only intended to give you a general idea of how much felt is necessary to make each puppet.

GLOVES

Plain canvas or jersey knit work and sport gloves with rib-knit wrist cuffs are recommended. Though you will find gloves with rubberized fingertips, suede inserts, and gloves made from pastel or printed fabrics, purchase the plainest gloves you can find (off-white canvas or brown). The knit cuffs will vary in color, but that won't matter. Even if you have a small hand, it is recommended that you buy men's-size gloves. A snugly fitting glove will be more difficult to put on and remove. Also, the larger finger size will give you more surface for displaying miniature puppet details, such as clothing, props, and scenery. A good alternative to buying gloves is to make your own gloves from felt. This will give you a wide variety of background colors to choose from and a smoother overall surface (see pattern provided on page 18).

GLUE

Elmer's Glue

Use Elmer's glue for gluing interfacing stick-puppet figures to posterboard. Since it soaks into cloth and dries stiff, it makes cutting the finished puppet easier. It should *not* be used on any other puppet projects in this book.

White Craft Glue

The extra thick or super tacky type that dries clear and flexible is the best for these activities and can be found in craft stores.

Hot Glue

This is necessary for some of the larger, heavier puppets. It's also great for gluing pom-poms to glove fingers. If you don't already own a hot-glue gun, invest in a sturdy, standard-size that has a trigger for dispensing. The miniature glue guns and those with no trigger can be frustrating and a waste of your time, money, and effort. Hot-glue guns and glue sticks can be found in craft and hardware stores, as well as most discount stores.

MARKERS

These should also be purchased in a craft or art supply store. You will need one set of assorted-colored, permanent (not water soluble) markers, and one set of assorted-colored, water-based markers. All markers should have a fine or ultra fine point so the small details on the stick puppets will maintain their clarity. All stick-puppet patterns should be traced onto interfacing with a permanent black art marker. This clearly outlines each figure and makes it easy to see from a distance. Don't use a ballpoint pen when tracing on interfacing.

MINIATURES

Many of the flat items made from patterns can be replaced by realistic, three-dimensional miniatures. Miniatures can be found in craft stores and stores where dollhouse supplies are sold. Send away for catalogs of dollhouse supplies to locate additional sources. Using three-dimensional objects gives a professional look to your puppet presentations. It is truly worth the time and effort spent in finding them. Buy with future projects in mind. For example, when you find small hats you would like to use, don't buy just one hat. Buy two or three hats saving you trips back and forth to the store. And you won't run the risk of the specific items you need being out of stock later when you need them. Listed here are some examples of available and highly recommended items.

Hats

Both men's and women's styles are available, and many of these are perfectly sized for pom-pom puppet heads. Among the most common are felt bowlers, top hats, cowboy hats, sailor hats, clown hats, baseball caps, straw farmers' hats, and a variety of straw ladies' hats which can be embellished with tiny flowers, bows, lace, and satin ribbons.

Cake Decorations and Party Favors

Included among these are such items as umbrellas, fans, baby bottles, plastic safety pins, spiders, plastic balloons, and award ribbons.

Dollhouse Miniatures

You will find all kinds of miniature food items, kitchen utensils, garden tools, candlesticks, animals, toys, furniture, musical instruments, and baskets. The possibilities are endless.

NOSES

Black, plastic animal noses with stems are available in a variety of sizes. Heart-shaped, bear, koala, and button noses are also available, but mostly in larger sizes. If the recommended animal nose cannot be found, substitute felt shapes or black pom-poms.

PAINT

Acrylic paint is best for these activities. It is odorless and dries quickly, unlike oil paint. It does not fade, peel, chip, or water-spot like watercolors or poster paint. Clean-up is quick and easy because you can just wash the brushes in dishwashing liquid and water and rinse thoroughly. Acrylic paint comes in tubes, bottles, and jars of varying sizes and there is an array of colors from which to choose. For small areas and details, apply the paint by dipping the brush directly into the container. For larger jobs, such as painting paper plates, squeeze or pour paint into a paper bowl and thin the paint with water until it is the consistency of heavy cream.

There are many special types of paints that can add to puppet details. Pearlescent, iridescent, slick, glitter, metallic, and puff paint are just a few. Many of these paints come in tubes. Use the tubes like pens for painting lines or squeeze the paint from the tube and apply it with a brush to cover large areas. Try using glitter pens, liquid glitter, or fashion-stamp tints to create unusual visual effects.

PAINTBRUSHES

Buy brushes designed for acrylic paint at a craft or art supply store. Inexpensive paintbrushes lose their bristles, which can be annoying and time-consuming when you're constantly stopping to pick stray bristles off projects. You'll need a 1 1/2-inch (3.9 cm) to 2-inch (5.0 cm) flat brush, round #6 or #7 brush, round #4 or #5 brush, and a round #1 or #2 brush for fine details. Be careful not to let paint dry in the bristles. Reshape the round brushes into a pointed tip between your thumb and forefinger after each washing so the bristles will dry in the proper shape.

PAPER PLATES

Paper plates come in an endless array of styles, sizes, and prices. The sturdiest (and most expensive) are found in card shops and party supply stores. However, some supermarkets carry sturdy brands. The plain white paper plates that can be bought in bulk are often quite flimsy, but you can strengthen them by gluing two or more together. These are the least expensive and are sufficient for most of the paper-plate puppets. Do not use the pressed board, plastic, or foam plates because they tear too easily.

INTERFACING

Interfacing glued to posterboard is what most of the stick puppets are made from. Interfacing is a non-woven material sold in fabric stores and is used primarily for stiffening fabrics. It comes in several different weights, thicknesses, and colors. The ideal type of interfacing for the puppets is medium-weight white. It is stiff enough to retain its shape, yet thin enough to see through to trace the patterns. Interfacing is an excellent surface which can be colored with crayons, art markers, colored pencils, or even paint. It is best to purchase interfacing from bolts by the yard. Lightweight and prepackaged interfacing is usually too flimsy, and heavyweight interfacing may be difficult to trace through. Test the different weights by feeling them and holding a pattern beneath them. You'll be able to determine which is best for your needs.

POM-POMS

Acrylic pom-poms come in a wide variety of colors. Sizes ranges from 3 mm to 2 inches (5.0 cm). Specific sizes and colors are recommended for each pom-pom puppet project. If these are unavailable, the next size either larger or smaller would be an acceptable substitute. The face and ear patterns are scaled to the recommended pom-pom size, so if you do make substitutes, simply adjust the patterns accordingly. Pom-poms can be found at most craft, fabric, and some discount stores. If you are unable to find a particular size or color, make felt circles the size and color you need.

POSTERBOARD

Though posterboard comes in many thicknesses and colors, 6-ply white posterboard is recommended for all the stick puppets in these activities. You can obtain posterboard at most craft or art supply stores. It is thick enough to be durable, yet is still relatively easy to cut with scissors. Oaktag is usually too flimsy to make a durable stick puppet. Four-ply posterboard is recommended for the folded flaps that will be taped inside each puppet box.

RIBBON

The most commonly used ribbon is #9 ribbon. It is 1 1/2 inches (3.9 cm) wide and comes in a wonderful array of colors and tiny prints. It is perfect for pom-pom puppet clothing, hats, curtains, and other small features. Ribbon doesn't unravel when cut and the prints provide a colorful and eye-pleasing contrast to the solid colors. Ribbon can be found in most craft and fabric stores, as well as some discount stores.

SCISSORS

Even if you already own a pair of scissors, invest in a good pair of 8-inch (20.3 cm) sewing scissors and a scissors sharpener. Use these scissors for all your puppet and craft projects. If you keep them sharpened (especially after cutting paper or posterboard), they will serve you well for many years and you'll be able to cut posterboard easily and cleanly.

STRAWS

Straight, clear, plastic drinking straws are best for these activities. Striped ones can be used as an alternative, but don't use the straws that have a section that bends.

TAPE

The best tape for these activities is book tape. It comes in 2-inch (5.0 cm) and 4-inch (10.2 cm) widths and can be found in most office supply stores. It is fairly expensive, but it is thick and strong and worth the price. Unlike Scotch tape, book tape does not crack, dry out, discolor, or lose its stickiness, even after years of use and exposure to temperature extremes. Book tape is also perfect for sealing or laminating small paper puppets. An acceptable substitute for book tape is clear package-sealing tape.

VELCRO ADHESIVE

This adhesive is used to glue Velcro to fabric surfaces, such as interfacing and garden gloves. If you use any other kind of glue, the Velcro will eventually peel off with use. Velcro adhesive can be found in fabric and craft stores.

PRESENTATION BOX

MATERIALS

- cardboard box or grocery carton (15" x 18" x 8") (38.1 cm x 45.7 cm x 20.3 cm) with flaps attached
- posterboard
- book tape

1. Fold the flaps down inside the box and tape the flaps in place.

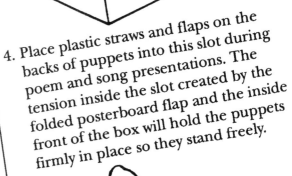

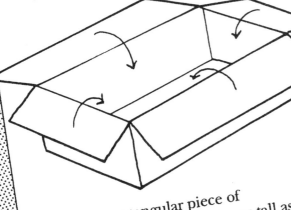

2. Cut a rectangular piece of posterboard almost twice as tall as the height of the box and 2 inches (5.0 cm) narrower than the box's longest side.

3. Fold the posterboard in half lengthwise and place it (fold side up) inside the box against one of the box's long sides. Tape the posterboard in place along the bottom and up the sides. This will create a slot between the box and the posterboard flap.

4. Place plastic straws and flaps on the backs of puppets into this slot during poem and song presentations. The tension inside the slot created by the folded posterboard flap and the inside front of the box will hold the puppets firmly in place so they stand freely.

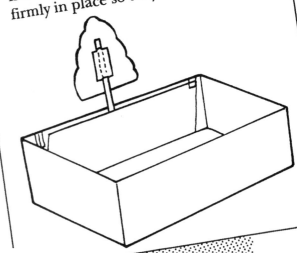

BASIC PUPPET ASSEMBLY
TECHNIQUES

The making of many of these puppets may seem to be time-consuming. These puppets were designed to be easy to make. But extra help is always welcome. Invite adult volunteers to help you construct the puppets, if you wish. Or, you can team up with other teachers and share the puppet-making and presentations with your classes. You may want to ask the help of other children in the school as well.

GLOVE PUPPETS

Loaded with whimsical charm and child appeal, these puppets can bring an endless array of familiar nursery rhymes and fingerplays to life. Glue the pom-poms to the back or fingernail side of the glove fingers. To begin each presentation, fold your gloved fingers down in a fist with the back of your fist facing the audience. The puppets are hidden from view to maintain the element of surprise until each finger pops up. This technique also makes it easier to put on and remove the gloves when performing two-handed presentations. There will be a few exceptions to this rule, which are indicated in the individual instructions for each puppet.

Before making a glove puppet, look closely at the glove. Notice the seams running around the outside of the finger edges. Try a glove on, spread your fingers, and look at the back of your gloved hand. The glove seam should be running right through the middle of the thumb surface. This is the surface to which you will glue the thumb pom-pom.

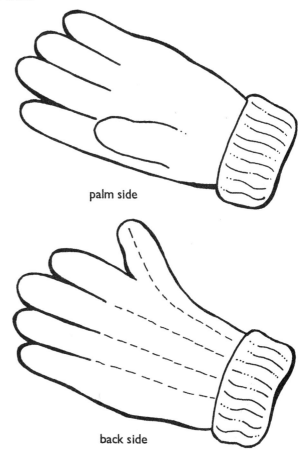

palm side

back side

To maintain this surface position for gluing, pinch the glove thumb together with your other hand and remove the glove. Glue all the pom-poms to the glove finger-tips.

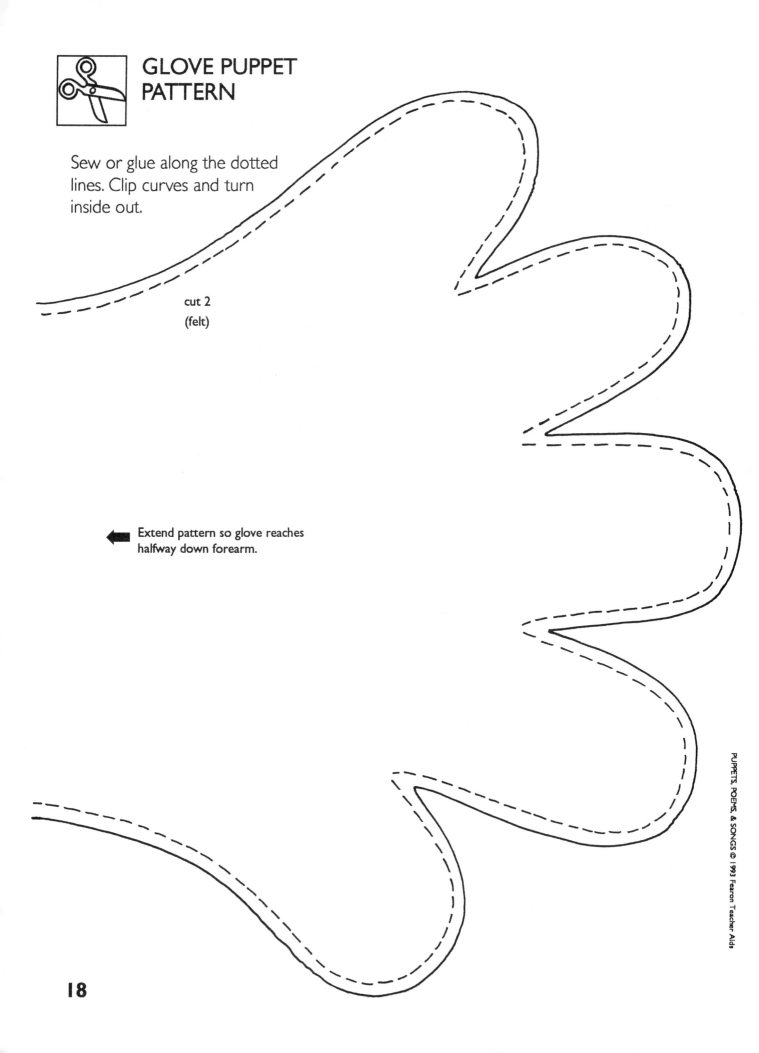

GLOVE PUPPET PATTERN

Sew or glue along the dotted lines. Clip curves and turn inside out.

cut 2
(felt)

Extend pattern so glove reaches halfway down forearm.

PUPPETS, POEMS, & SONGS © 1993 Fearon Teacher Aids

PEOPLE PUPPETS

Several glove puppets feature people on the fingertips. Several patterns are provided on pages 22 and 23. The following are instructions for making a girl, a boy, a woman, and a man.

Girl

1. Cut the bottom front half of a pom-pom ($^{1}/_{2}$-inch or 1-inch) (1.3 cm or 2.5 cm) flat with scissors.

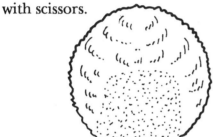

2. Cut a girl's face (see child's face pattern on page 22) from skin-tone felt.
3. Glue the felt face to the trimmed flat surface of the pom-pom with the chin extending down below the bottom.
4. Pull the pom-pom fibers forward over the top edge of the face and glue lightly into place for bangs.

5. To make long hair, glue a 4 $^{1}/_{2}$-inch (11.4 cm) long clump of embroidery thread to each side of the face. When the glue is dry, tie each clump with a ribbon. You may add bows, barrettes, or headbands to long or short hair, if you wish.

6. Cut a dress and arms (see patterns on page 23) from #9 calico ribbon. You may decide to cut pants and a shirt instead.
7. Cut hands (page 22) from the same color felt as the face. Glue the hands to the ends of the arms (page 22) on the back side of the arm fabric.

8. Glue the arms to the back of the dress or shirt.

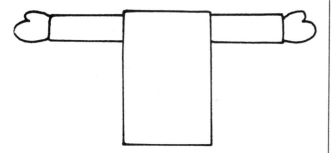

9. Glue the dress or pants and shirt to the glove finger under the head pom-pom. Bring the arms forward and glue the hands to the front of the shirt or dress. Or, if the puppet is holding something, glue the hands and arms in a natural position for holding that particular object.

10. Decorate the neckline, hemline, and dress or shirt sleeves with narrow trims, such as rickrack, lace, or braid.

Variation for Woman

Follow the directions for the child puppet, but use a 1 ½-inch (3.9 cm) or 2-inch (5.0 cm) pom-pom and the larger face pattern (page 22). Bring the pom-pom fibers down over the forehead. Glue two wiggly eyes (6 to 8 mm) in place.

Boy

1. Cut the bottom front half of a pom-pom (½-inch or 1-inch) (1.3 cm or 2.5 cm) flat with scissors.

2. Cut the boy's face (see child's face pattern on page 22) from skin-tone felt.
3. Glue the felt face to the trimmed flat surface of the pom-pom with the chin extending down below the bottom.
4. Pull the pom-pom fibers forward over the top edge of the face and glue lightly into place for bangs.

5. Cut pants, shirt, and vest (see patterns on page 23) from felt.

6. Clip the shirt along the dotted line and fold each corner forward to make a collar.

7. Glue the vest in place on the shirt.

8. Cut the arms and hands from the same color felt as the face. Glue the hands to the ends of the arms.

9. Glue the arms to the back of the shirt.

10. Glue the pants and shirt to the glove finger under the head pom-pom. Bring the arms forward and glue the hands to the front of the shirt. Or, if the puppet is holding something, glue the hands and arms in a natural position for holding that particular object.

Variation for Man

Cut the man's face (see pattern on page 22) from skin-tone felt. Draw a line of glue down the center. Pinch the line of glue together to make a crease down the center of the face for a nose. Glue the face to a 2-inch (5.0 cm) pom-pom with the crease running vertically. Glue wiggly eyes (6 to 8 mm) to the face on either side of the nose crease.

PEOPLE PUPPET PATTERNS

child's face
(use 1 1/2-inch (3.9 cm) pom-pom)

child's hand
cut 2
(skin-tone felt)

arm
cut 2

adult's hand
cut 2
(skin-tone felt)

man's face
(use 2-inch (5.0 cm) pom-pom)

woman's face
(use 1 1/2-inch (3.9 cm) pom-pom)

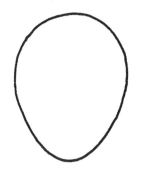

woman's face
(use 2-inch (5.0 cm) pom-pom)

PUPPETS, POEMS, & SONGS © 1993 Fearon Teacher Aids

PEOPLE PUPPET PATTERNS

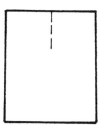

child's shirt

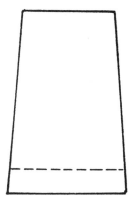

dress
(adjust length as desired)

child's pants

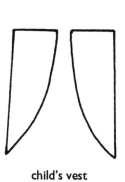

child's vest

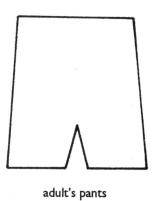

adult's pants

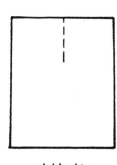

adult's shirt

BASIC PUPPET ASSEMBLY TECHNIQUES

STICK PUPPETS

1. Place interfacing on top of the patterns and trace the patterns onto the interfacing with a black permanent marker.
2. Color the figures with crayons, pressing firmly so the colors will be vivid. (Always color the interfacing figures before cutting them out. The extra material gives you something to hold on to while coloring and you can use the extra space for testing color combinations.)
3. Cut the figures apart so each is on its own separate piece of interfacing, but do not cut along the figure outlines yet.

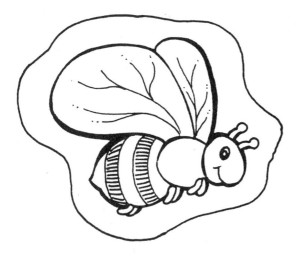

4. Turn the interfacing figure over so the back is facing up. Using Elmer's glue, trace along the outer lines of the puppet with a line of glue. Smooth and spread the glue slightly with your fingertip. It isn't necessary to spread the glue over the entire figure.
5. Turn the puppet over and glue it to the posterboard. (Always color interfacing figures *before* gluing to the posterboard. When the glue soaks through the interfacing, its surface texture changes, which

drastically and adversely affects its colorability.) Let the glue dry thoroughly.
6. Cut the figures out. Small white areas (such as spaces between arms and legs) can either be left in place or cut out with an X-acto knife.
7. Using book tape, attach a plastic drinking straw to the back of each of the figures. The straw should extend several inches below the bottom edge of the puppet. The tape should begin at least an inch above the bottom edge of the puppet so the puppet will overlap the box edge when the straw is placed in the box stage slot.

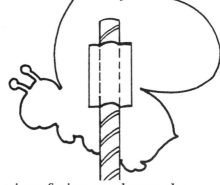

8. The interfacing overlay on the posterboard stick puppets helps make the puppets stronger and more durable. However, if extensions, such as arms or legs, become bent or fragile, reinforce them by gluing a length of a bamboo skewer to the back of the puppet.

TIPS FOR COLORING INTERFACING

1. Press firmly with crayons. Although the rough-textured interfacing will wear down the crayons quickly, the results will be eye-catchingly visible from the back of the room.

2. Blend colors and create textures. Keep in mind that nothing in nature is exactly the same shade. A pink pig might also have shadows and highlights of orange, yellow, or even purple. Shade a white goose with gray or brown or add yellow and gold highlights. For a furry animal, select one shade of brown to be the basic color. Then try rough-stroking short lines over the basic color with several different shades of brown to give the illusion of fur. Add subtle touches of gray, black, orange, and yellow. Vary the basic brown shades from animal to animal within each story to give your figures more contrast, greater individuality, and more visual appeal. By highlighting and blending colors and by combining crayons and art markers for shading and contrast, you will give your puppets the illusion of roundness and depth and a more realistic, textured appearance.

3. Don't hesitate to use white. It isn't necessary for every space to be covered with color. Use white as a highlight to brighten up a dark figure. Also, a white apron, shirt, cap, or socks make an appealing and desired contrast with the rest of the colors.

CUP PUPPETS

1. Cut the cover pattern (see page 26) from felt to fit the cup you're using.
2. Glue the cover to the outside of the cup, with the bottom edges even and the excess felt extending up above the top of the cup.

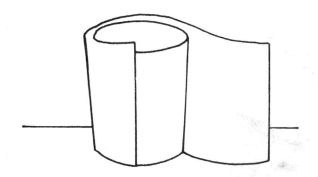

3. Fold the excess felt down inside the cup and glue in place.

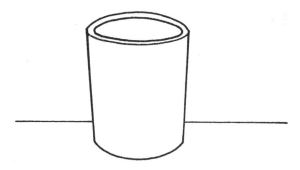

PUPPET MANIPULATOR

1. Fold two 1 1/2-inch (3.9 cm) pieces of tape in half lengthwise with the sticky side out.
2. Place one piece of tape on the back of the puppet head, with the folded edge just above the center.
3. Place a straw in the center of the sticky tape with the straw tip close to the cardboard head, but not quite touching it (see page 27).
4. Place the second piece of tape about 1/4 inch (6 mm) above the first so the folded edges are parallel.
5. Press the tape pieces together with the straw between them. The tape acts as a hinge, which enables you to push the puppet up out of its "home" with the straw (illustrated on page 27).

CUP COVER
PATTERN

PUPPETS, POEMS, & SONGS © 1993 Fearon Teacher Aids

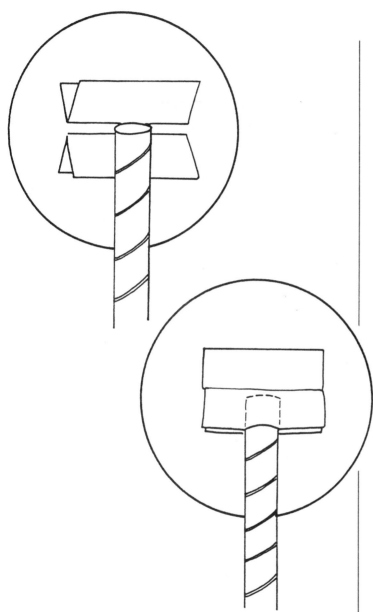

PAPER-PLATE PUPPETS

There are three types of paper-plate puppets—those folded in half and held in the hand, those in which the hand is inserted between the plates, and those mounted on a stick or rod. The latter two will be explained here.

Paper-Plate Hand Puppets

Staple two paper plates together around the edges leaving an unstapled area at the bottom that is large enough to insert your hand.

Plate Stick Puppet

1. Tape a paint stick to the unpainted side of the plate that will be used as the back of the puppet head. (Wooden paint-stirring sticks are the best for this activity. You may also use wooden dowels or cardboard paper-towel tubes.) Adjust the stick to make the gripping area as long or as short as you like.

BASIC PUPPET ASSEMBLY TECHNIQUES

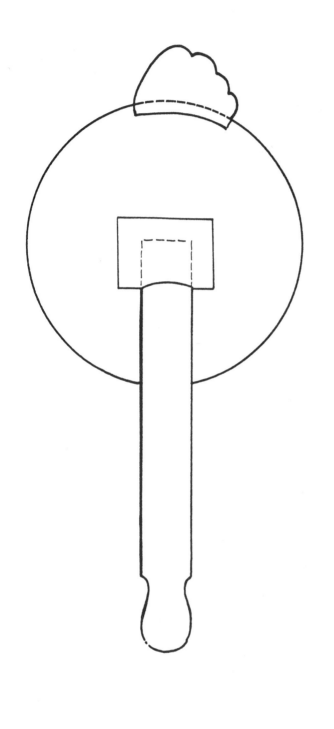

2. Position the face plate of the puppet over the back plate, making sure the face is aligned straight up and down with the stick. Staple the front plate to the back plate around the edges.

TIPS FOR A SUCCESSFUL
PRESENTATION

KNOW THE MATERIAL

Poems and songs rely on rhythm, cadence, and rhyme. Memorize the poems and songs word for word, so the words come automatically and a child's interrupting comment or question can be taken in stride.

BE FAMILIAR WITH THE PUPPETS

Learn to hold and manipulate the puppets with familiarity and expertise, while being mindful to coordinate the puppet's actions with the words of the poem or song so no surprises are given away too early. Sit in a comfortable chair with the box of puppets in your lap. They should be placed in the box face down, in reverse order of the way they will be presented (the last puppet on the bottom and the first one on top). Have another chair beside you on which to set the puppets you have finished using. Practice in front of a mirror and watch yourself as you present each poem or song.

BE THEATRICAL!

This vital element can make the difference between a flat, ho-hum performance and a performance that will dazzle and delight your audience and have them begging for more. I cannot stress this strongly enough. Don't simply recite the words to the children. Speak to the children as though you are telling them the world's most magical secrets. Don't simply display the puppets, interact with them. If a puppet pops up out of nowhere, react with surprise and pleasure. If puppets gradually disappear, react with growing dismay and consternation. A caterpillar turning into a butterfly is magic to a young child. Show that with your eyes, your face, and with awe and excitement in your voice. Exaggerate. Ham it up. Above all, don't be concerned about looking silly. Throw away

Tips For a Successful Presentation

your inhibitions and give your presentation everything you
have for a truly special effect. The more you enjoy what you
and your puppets are doing, the more your audience will
enjoy it, too.

THE BRINY DEEP

1. Make the box according to the instructions provided on page 16.
2. Cover the outside of the box with blue felt.
3. With paint or permanent markers, draw wavy lines on the side of the box that will be facing the audience.

FIVE LITTLE FISHES

MATERIALS

- patterns (pages 34-36)
- garden glove
- felt
  brightly colored scraps
  pink (7" x 8") (17.7 cm x 20.3 cm)
  gray (12" x 15") (30.5 cm x 38.1 cm)
  white (3" x 12") (7.6 cm x 30.5 cm)
- 5 brightly colored pom-poms (1 1/2") (3.9 cm)
- 5 wiggly eyes (10 mm)
- 2 black buttons
- yarn (6") (15.2 cm)
- tagboard (7" x 8") (17.7 cm x 20.3 cm)

Fish Glove Puppet

1. Cut five fish tails and five fins (see patterns on page 34) from brightly colored felt (matching the pom-pom colors or contrasting with them).
2. Separating the pom-pom fibers, glue a fin to the top of each pom-pom and a tail to one side. (Fins should curve backwards towards the tails.)

3. Glue a curving bit of yarn for the mouth.
4. Glue a brightly colored pom-pom fish to the fingernail side of each glove fingertip. If you are using a right-handed glove, the fish should be facing toward your right when the glove is held up in the proper presentation position. This way, the fish will be facing away from the shark as the shark rises up from the box, and the fish will be heading in the right direction when they swim away behind your back. If you are using a left-handed glove, the fish should be facing toward your left.
5. Glue one eye on each pom-pom fish.

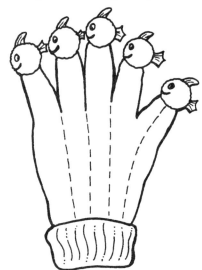

Shark Puppet

1. Cut one jaw (page 36) from pink felt and one jaw from tagboard. Glue the two pieces together.
2. Fold the jaw on the dotted line with the pink felt inside. The shorter side will be the lower jaw and the longer side will be the upper jaw.

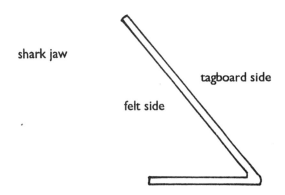

shark jaw

tagboard side

felt side

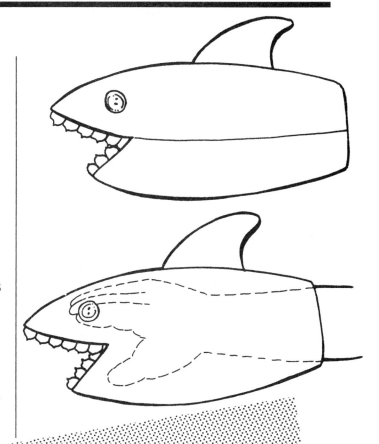

3. Cut the lower shark body (page 34), upper shark body (page 35), and two dorsal fins (page 36) from gray felt.

4. Glue the upper body to the tagboard side of the upper jaw around the edges only. Glue the lower body to the tagboard side of the lower jaw around the edges only.

5. Glue the body pieces together along the sides, leaving the end open for your hand.

6. Glue the two dorsal fins together leaving ³⁄₈ inch (1 cm) free on each flat end to make a tab. Glue the fin tab to the shark's back so the fin curves backwards towards the tail end.

7. Cut the teeth (page 36) from white felt and glue them to the upper and lower jaws.

8. Glue black button eyes to each side of the shark's head.

PUPPETS, POEMS, & SONGS © 1993 Fearon Teacher Aids

POEM

Five Little Fishes

One little fishy, swimming in the ocean blue.
(Hold up one gloved finger at a time as indicated.)
Here comes another one, now there are two.
Two little fishes swimming in the sea,
Here comes another one, now there are three.
Three little fishes, swimming near the shore.
Here comes another one, now there are four.

Four little fishes swim around and dive.
Here comes another one, now there are five.
(Bring your other hand with the shark puppet up out of the box and swim the shark around, gradually moving the shark closer and closer to the fish.)
Here comes a shark, looking for some fun.
Look out, little fishes!
And away they run.
(Swim the fish behind your back.)

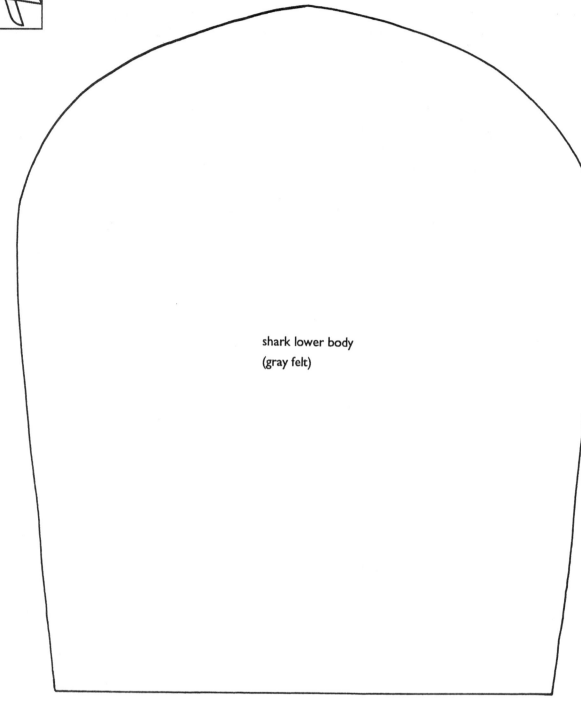

shark lower body
(gray felt)

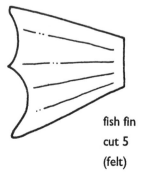

fish fin
cut 5
(felt)

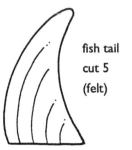

fish tail
cut 5
(felt)

34

PUPPETS, POEMS, & SONGS © 1993 Fearon Teacher Aids

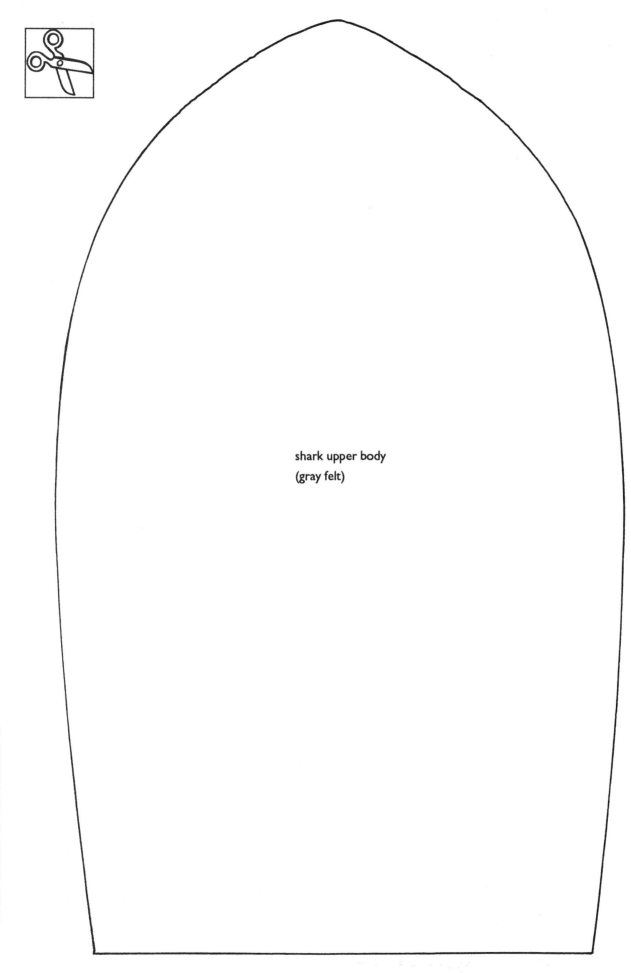

shark upper body
(gray felt)

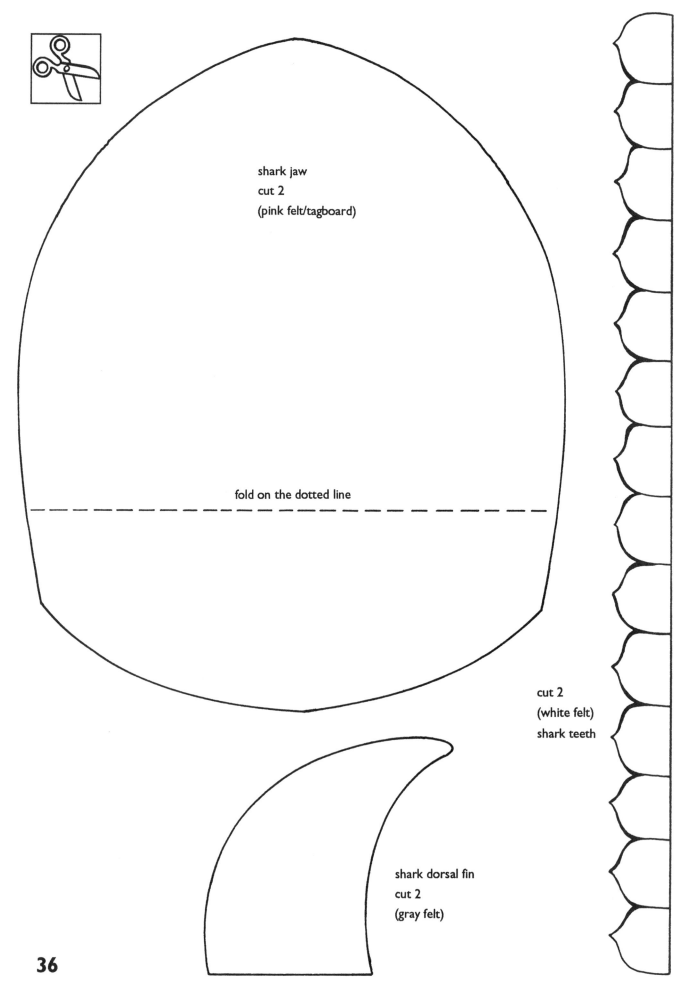

shark jaw
cut 2
(pink felt/tagboard)

fold on the dotted line

cut 2
(white felt)
shark teeth

shark dorsal fin
cut 2
(gray felt)

36

A JELLYFISH LIVES IN THE OCEAN

MATERIALS

- fish pattern (page 39)
- 2 paper plates (7") (17.7 cm)
- paper bowl
- iridescent paint
- wiggly eyes
  6 (7 mm)
  2 (20 mm)
- hole punch
- iridescent gift-wrap ribbon
- construction-paper scraps (various colors)
- markers
- book tape

Jellyfish Paper-Bowl Puppet

1. Paint the bottoms of two paper plates as well as the bottom of a paper bowl. Let the paint dry thoroughly.
2. Punch holes around the edge of one paper plate. Thread varying lengths of narrow ribbon through the holes so the ribbons hang down like long tentacles. Curl some of the ribbons and leave some hanging loosely. Tape the ribbons securely to the unpainted side of the plate. This will completely seal the surface with tape and your fingers will not snag on loops of ribbon when you insert your hand into the finished puppet.
3. Glue the inverted bowl to the painted side of the second paper plate. Staple the two plates together around the edges, leaving enough area unstapled to insert your hand.
4. Glue two wiggly eyes (20 mm) to the front side of the bowl, opposite the opening for your hand.

5. Cut five little fish (page 39) from construction paper. Draw scales and other details on both sides of the fish with markers.

6. Cover each fish with book tape. Glue a wiggly eye (7 mm) to both sides of each fish and tape the fish to the tentacles.

A Jellyfish Lives in the Ocean
(Tune: "My Bonnie Lies Over the Ocean")

A jellyfish lives in the ocean.
(Bring the jellyfish up out of the box.)
A jellyfish lives in the sea.
A jellyfish eats little fishes.
(Indicate the fish hanging from the tentacles.)
I hope that he doesn't eat me.
Float on, float on,

Float on and float on, little jellyfish.
Float on, float on,
Float on little jellyfish.
(Jerk the jellyfish sharply upward and lower gently throughout the chorus to imitate the way a jellyfish moves.)

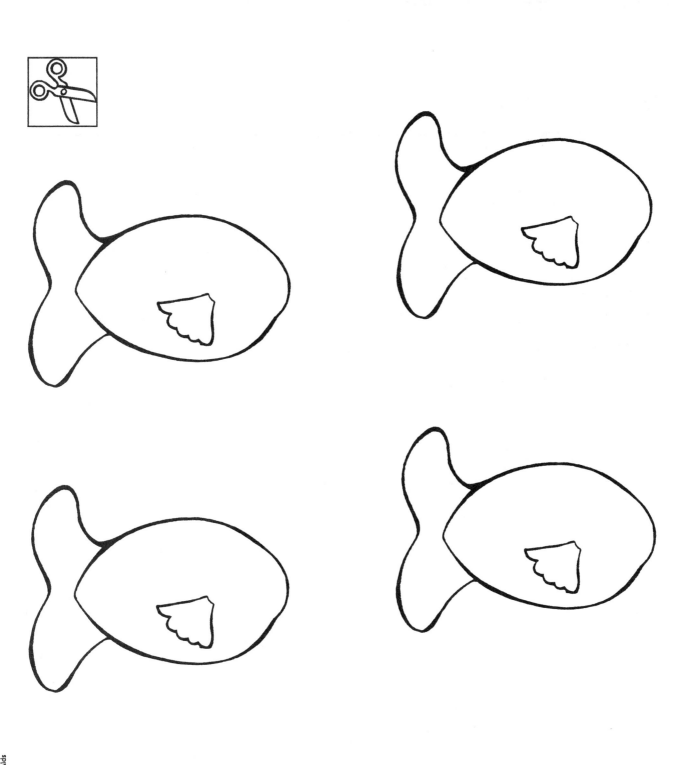

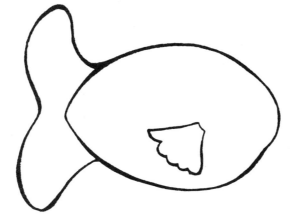

AN OCTOPUS IS SLEEPING

MATERIALS

- patterns (page 42)
- felt scraps
  red
  black
- 2 lunch-size paper bags
- black construction-paper scrap
- 2 wiggly eyes (35 mm)

Octopus Paper-Bag Puppet

1. Cut two eyelids (page 42) from black felt.
2. Cut two eyelashes (page 42) from black construction paper. Fringe and curl the rounded edges.
3. Glue the eyelashes around the rounded edge of the felt eyelids.
4. Cut a mouth (page 42) from red felt and glue the mouth to the center of a paper bag.
5. Lift the bottom flap of the bag and glue the wiggly eyes underneath.
6. Glue the eyelids (with the eyelashes attached) to the top of the bag flap so that the eyelids and lashes hang over the edge of the flap slightly. Be sure the wiggly eyes are concealed by the eyelids until the flap is raised.

7. Cut eight strips from the second lunch bag, each as long as the length of the bag and 1 1/4 inches (3.1 cm) wide. Glue three of the strips to the bottom of the octopus bag across the front. Glue three strips across the back. Then glue one strip on each side.

8. Insert your hand into the bag, curling your fingers down over the edge into the flap. Straighten your fingers to raise the flap and reveal the eyes.

An Octopus Is Sleeping

An octopus is sleeping at the bottom of the sea.
(Hold up the paper-bag octopus with the eyes closed.)
Her eyes are closed up tightly,
She can't see you or me.
But if she senses danger,
Her eyes will open wide.
(Raise the bag flap suddenly to reveal the eyes.)
Then she'll quickly swim away
Back to her hole to hide.
(Swim the octopus behind your back.)

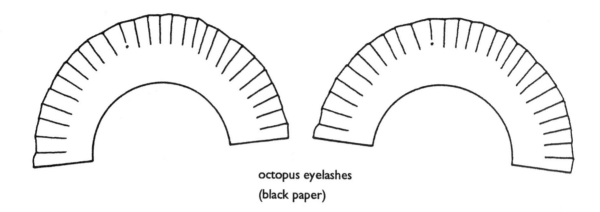

octopus eyelashes
(black paper)

octopus eyelids
(black felt)

octopus mouth
(red felt)

FIVE LITTLE SEASHELLS

MATERIALS

- patterns (pages 45 and 46)
- garden glove
- interfacing (10" x 10") (25.4 cm x 25.4 cm)
- posterboard (8" x 10") (20.3 cm x 25.4 cm)
- black permanent marker
- crayons
- dowel
- book tape

Seashell Glove Puppet

1. Using a black marker, trace five seashells (page 45) onto interfacing.
2. Color and cut the seashells out.
3. Glue a seashell to the fingernail side of each glove fingertip. (You may want to glue real seashells instead of pattern shapes.)

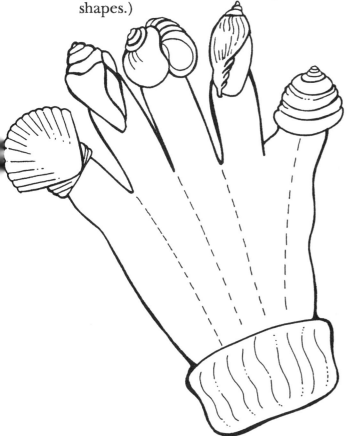

Wave Stick Puppet

1. Using a black marker, trace the wave (page 46) onto interfacing.
2. Color and glue the wave to posterboard and then cut the wave out.
3. Tape a dowel or paint stick to the back of the wave with book tape.

POEM

PUPPETS, POEMS, & SONGS © 1993 Fearon Teacher Aids

Five Little Seashells

Five little seashells
On the sandy shore.
(Hold up all five gloved fingers.)
WHOOSH! comes a great big wave.
(Move the wave puppet in front of
the gloved hand with a slow,
smooth curving motion. While the
glove is temporarily hidden behind
the wave, lower one finger, then
move the wave to reveal that one
seashell is missing. Repeat this
process as the rhyme progresses.)

Now there are four!
Four little seashells lying by the sea.
WHOOSH! comes a great big wave,
now there are three!
Three little seashells by the ocean
blue.
WHOOSH! comes a great big wave,
now there are two!
Two little seashells sleeping in the
sun.
WHOOSH! comes a great big wave,
now there's just one!
One little seashell, feeling all alone.
WHOOSH! comes a great big wave,
now there are none!

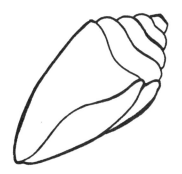

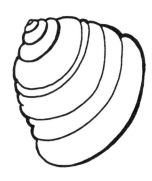

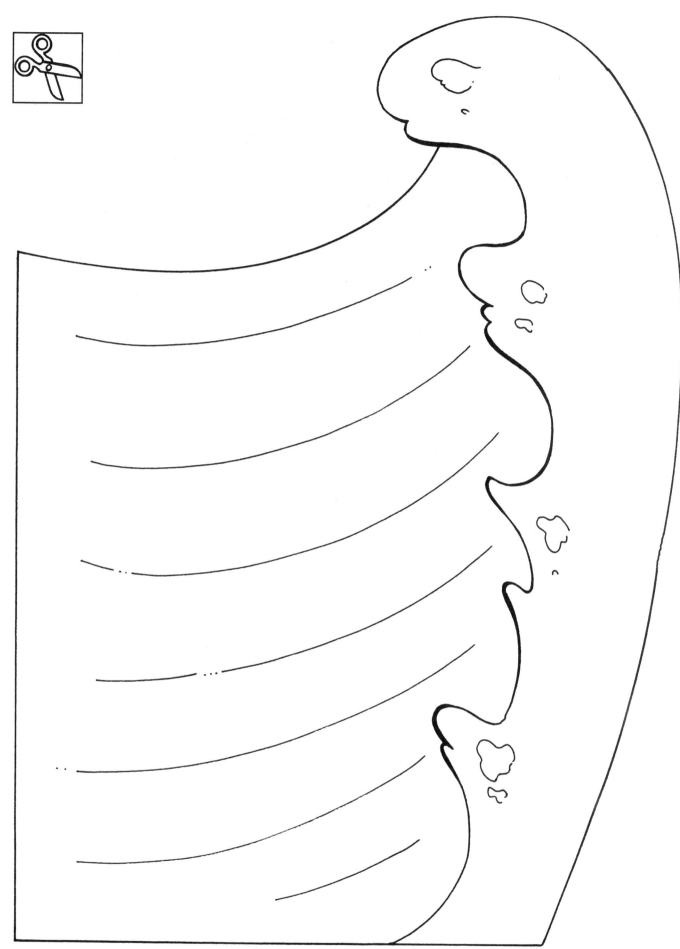

CLAMS CAN'T DANCE

MATERIALS

- paper plate (9") (22.9 cm)
- felt
  pink (9" x 18") (22.9 cm x 45.7 cm)
  white scrap
- 2 black button eyes
- fiberfill

Clam Paper-Plate Puppet

1. Cut two 8-inch (20.3 cm) circles from pink felt.
2. Placing the two circles on top of one another, glue or sew the edges together halfway around.

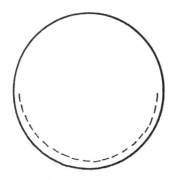

3. Turn the material inside out and stuff the glued or sewn half lightly with fiberfill.
4. Fold a paper plate in half with the bottom side out.
5. Place the opening of the stuffed felt semicircle on the fold inside the paper plate. The stuffed body will be sticking straight up in the center of the plate.
6. Glue the outer edges (unstuffed portion) of the felt semicircles to the plate semicircles.

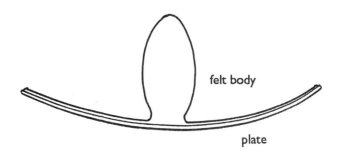

felt body

plate

7. Cut two ¹/₂" x 3" (1.3 cm x 7.6 cm) strips of white felt.
8. Glue both ends of one strip to the top of the clamshell and both ends of the other strip to the bottom. Leave the middle of each strip unglued to insert two fingers under the top strip and the thumb under the bottom strip to manipulate the puppet.
9. Sew or glue black button eyes to the front of the pink clam body.

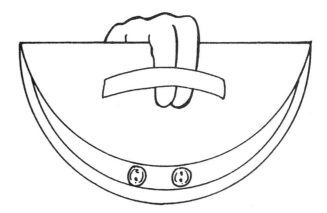

PUPPETS, POEMS, & SONGS © 1993 Fearon Teacher Aids

POEM

Clams Can't Dance

Clams can't dance.
(Hold up the clam puppet.)
And clams can't sing.
But clams are kind of neat.
They make a special music
By blowing bubbles to the beat!

(Sing the following to the tune of
"The Pink Panther," making soft,
explosive sounds through your lips
on each "p." Open and close the
clam shell as you sing).
Baloop, baloop,
Baloop-a-loop!

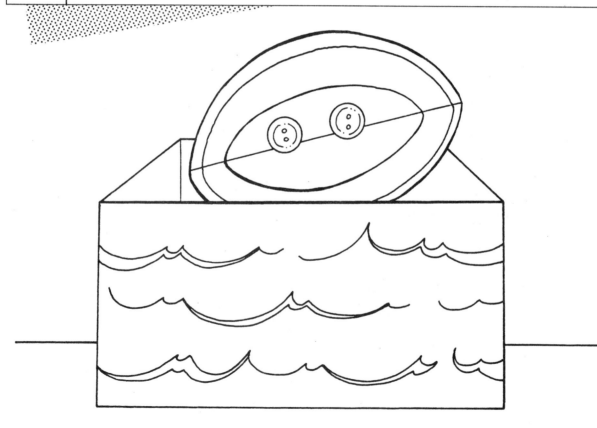

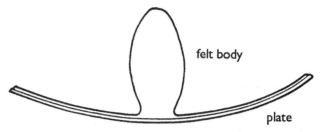

felt body

plate

OLGA OYSTER

MATERIALS

- eye patterns (page 50)
- paper plate (7") (17.7 cm)
- felt
  gray (7" x 14") (17.7 cm x 35.5 cm)
  black scraps
  white scraps
- dark gray paint
- large pearl
- fiberfill

Oyster Paper-Plate Puppet

1. Paint the bottom of a paper plate dark gray. Let the paint dry thoroughly.
2. Cut two 6-inch (15.2 cm) circles from gray felt.
3. Placing the two circles on top of one another, glue or sew the edges together halfway around.

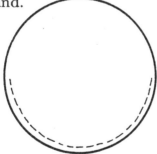

4. Turn the material inside out and stuff the glued or sewn half lightly with fiberfill.
5. Fold the painted paper plate in half with the gray side out.
6. Place the opening of the stuffed felt semicircle on the fold inside the paper plate. The stuffed body will be sticking straight up in the center.
7. Glue the outer edges (unstuffed portion) of the felt semicircles to the plate semicircles.

8. Cut two ¹/₂" x 3" (1.3 cm x 7.6 cm) strips of gray felt.
9. Glue both ends of one strip to the top of the oyster and both ends of the other strip to the bottom. Leave the middle of each strip unglued to insert two fingers under the top strip and the thumb under the bottom strip to manipulate the puppet.

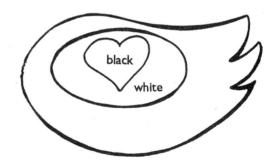

10. Cut two oyster eyes (page 50) from black and white felt.

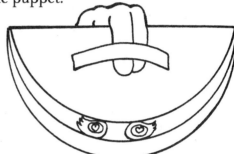

black

white

11. Glue the eyes to the oyster puppet.
12. Place a large pearl inside the puppet, beneath the puppet body, against the fold in the back of the plate.

The Briny Deep

POEM

PUPPETS, POEMS, & SONGS © 1993 Fearon Teacher Aids

Olga Oyster

Olga Oyster ate some sand.
(Hold up the oyster.)
It made poor Olga sick.
Olga Oyster ate some sand.
It made her go, "Hic! Hic!"
(Jerk the puppet as if it has the
hiccups.)

But Olga Oyster had a plan.
She's such a clever girl.
She covered up that scratchy sand
And made a lovely pearl!
(Reach into the shell beneath the
oyster and pull out the pearl.)

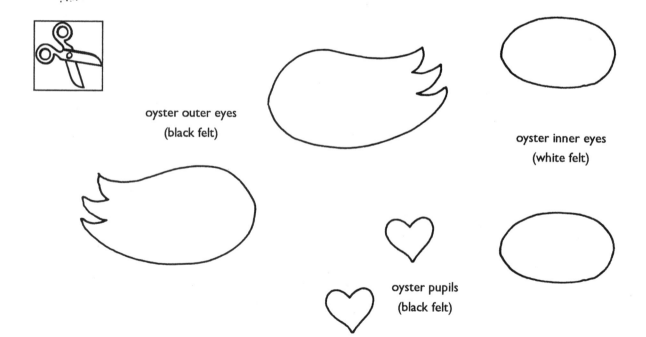

oyster outer eyes
(black felt)

oyster inner eyes
(white felt)

oyster pupils
(black felt)

PUPPETS, POEMS, & SONGS © 1993 Fearon Teacher Aids

A GOLDEN FISH

MATERIALS

- patterns (page 53)
- 3 paper plates (9") (22.9 cm)
- 2 wiggly eyes (20 mm) or black and white felt scraps
- orange or gold paint
- liquid gold glitter
- book tape

Fish Paper-Plate Puppet

1. Paint the bottoms of two paper plates and both sides of a third paper plate orange or gold. Let the paint dry thoroughly.
2. Trace and cut out one top fin, two side fins, and two tails (page 53) from the plate that is painted on both sides.
3. Staple the end of one tail to the unpainted side of one of the plates. Repeat by stapling the other tail to a second plate. Be sure both tails extend out from the plates the same distance.

4. Tape over the stapled ends of the tails to secure them completely. Your hand will fit into the paper-plate puppet between the two tails and you don't want any unsealed edges to catch on watches, rings, or clothing.
5. Fit the two plates together, painted sides out, with the tails matching. Position the top fin between the two plates and staple in place along the edges.
6. Staple all around the plate rim, except for the tail area. Leave enough space to fit your hand inside the plates between the two tails.
7. Glue on the eyes (page 53) and side fins. Sight along the edge of the plates from the front to make sure the eyes and fins are aligned opposite each other.
8. Paint the fins, tail, and scale lines with liquid gold glitter.

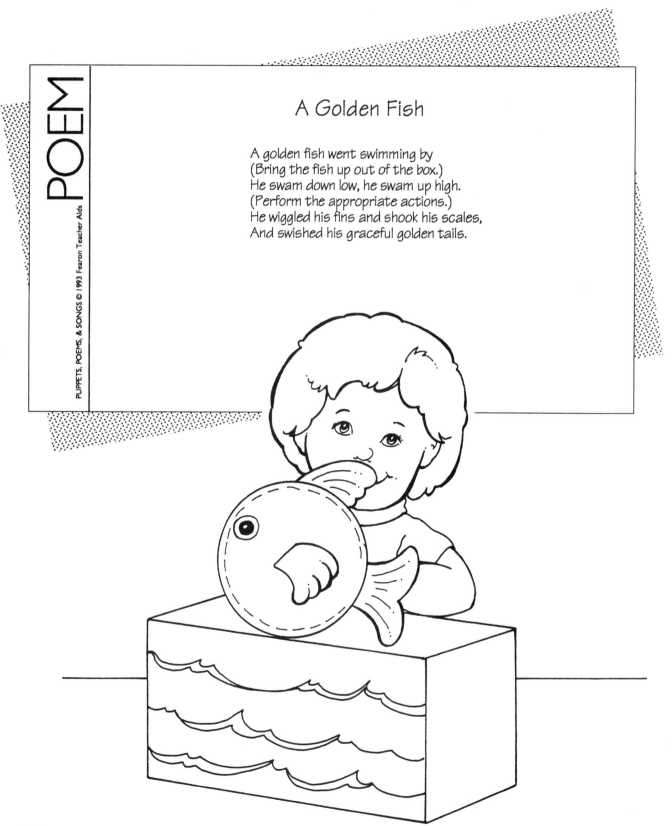

POEM

PUPPETS, POEMS, & SONGS © 1993 Fearon Teacher Aids

A Golden Fish

A golden fish went swimming by
(Bring the fish up out of the box.)
He swam down low, he swam up high.
(Perform the appropriate actions.)
He wiggled his fins and shook his scales,
And swished his graceful golden tails.

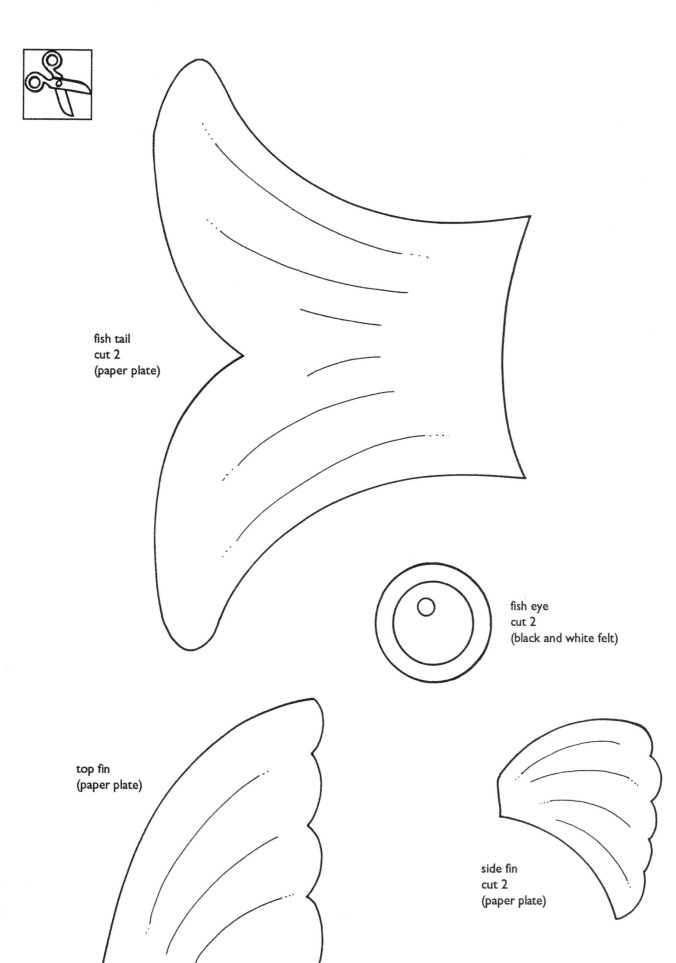

fish tail
cut 2
(paper plate)

fish eye
cut 2
(black and white felt)

top fin
(paper plate)

side fin
cut 2
(paper plate)

RUB-A-DUB-DUB

MATERIALS

- patterns (page 57)
- garden glove
- felt scraps
  white
  assorted colors
  skin-tone (4" x 6") (10.2 cm x 15.2 cm)
- 3 skin-tone pom-poms (5 mm)
- 6 wiggly eyes (7 mm)
- pipe cleaner
- interfacing scrap
- posterboard scrap
- black permanent marker
- crayons
- margarine tub
- fiberfill

Three Men

1. Cut the index finger and little finger off a garden glove where the fingers join the main body of the glove. Set the fingers aside.
2. Stuff the thumb and remaining two fingers lightly with fiberfill along the entire finger length.
3. Glue two wiggly eyes to the palm side of each of the stuffed fingers. Be sure to leave room above the eyes to attach little hats.
4. Glue one skin-tone pom-pom to the center of each finger, just below the eyes.

5. Cut three strips from the two removed glove fingers. Cut each strip the length of the finger and approximately 1 inch (2.5 cm) wide.
6. Cut a pipe cleaner into thirds. Place a pipe cleaner piece lengthwise along the middle of each strip. Fold both edges of the canvas over the pipe cleaner (you'll be folding each strip lengthwise into thirds) and glue into place. Cut the ends of the pipe cleaners even with the ends of the strips. These are the arms for each of the three finger puppets.

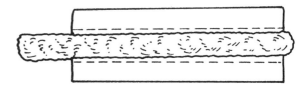

7. Glue one arm strip to the back of each finger puppet below the face, curving it forward around the sides. Glue each arm strip at the sides to retain the forward curve.
8. Cut six hands (page 57) from skin-tone felt. Glue them, thumbs up, to the ends of the arms.

Make One Man a Baker

1. Cut two baker's caps (page 57) from white felt.
2. Sew the two pieces together leaving the flat end open.
3. Turn the hat inside out and stuff the top half lightly with fiberfill.
4. Glue the hat to the head of the tallest glove finger.

5. Using a black marker, trace the cake pattern (page 57) onto interfacing. (You may want to use a miniature three-dimensional cake instead of the interfacing figure.)
6. Color and glue the cake to posterboard and then cut the cake out.
7. Glue the cake to the baker's hands.

Make One Man a Butcher

1. Cut two butcher's visors (page 57) from felt and glue them together.
2. Glue the curved edge of the visor to the thumb puppet's forehead.
3. Cut a very narrow strip of matching felt. Glue the strip around the back of the thumb puppet's head, connecting both edges of the visor.
4. Using a black marker, trace the cleaver and pork chop patterns (page 57) onto interfacing. (You may want to use miniature three-dimensional objects instead of the interfacing figures.)
5. Color and glue the figures to posterboard and then cut the figures out.
6. Glue the pork chop to the end of the cleaver and glue the cleaver to the butcher's right hand.

Make One Man a Candlestick Maker

1. Using a black marker, trace the candlestick pattern (page 57) onto interfacing. (You may want to use a miniature three-dimensional candlestick instead of the interfacing figure.)
2. Color and glue the candlestick to posterboard and then cut the candlestick out.

3. Curl the candlestick maker's outer hand around the candlestick and glue it in place.

Tub

1. Fit the ribbed cuff of the glove down over a small margarine tub.
2. Push the main body of the glove and the stuffed fingers down into the tub.
3. Arrange the finger puppets so they can all be seen, with the butcher in front, the baker on the left, and the candlestick maker on the right.

The Briny Deep

PUPPETS, POEMS, & SONGS © 1993 Fearon Teacher Aids

POEM

Rub-a-Dub-Dub

Three men in a tub
Rub-a-dub-dub
Three men in a tub,
(Rest the tub on the front edge of
the box.)
And who do you think they be?
The butcher, the baker,
The candlestick maker.
(Point to each in turn.)
And they all sailed out to sea.

(Sway the tub back and forth.)
These three wise men of Gotham
Sailed out to sea in their tub.
(Continue swaying the tub back and
forth, gradually lowering the tub into
the box.)
Uh-oh. Oh, dear
If their tub had been stronger,
This poem would be longer.
(Shrug.)

pork chop
(interfacing)

hand
cut 6
(skin-tone felt)

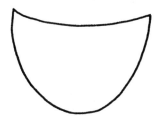

butcher's visor
cut 2
(black felt)

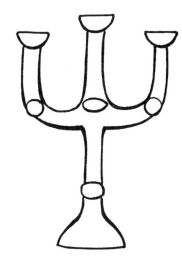

candlestick
(interfacing)

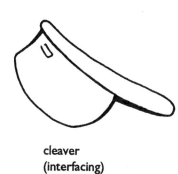

cleaver
(interfacing)

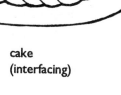

cake
(interfacing)

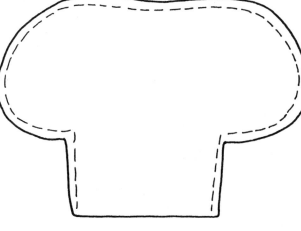

baker's cap
cut 2
(white felt)

CRABS A-WALKING

MATERIALS

- patterns (page 61)
- pair of garden gloves
- felt
  orange (24" x 36") (61 cm x 91.5 cm)
  red scrap
- 4 black button eyes
- carpet or buttonhole thread and needle
- fiberfill

Crab Glove Puppets

1. Cut an 8-inch (20.3 cm) circle from orange felt.
2. With carpet or buttonhole thread, stitch all around the circle ¹/₂ inch (1.3 cm) from the outer edge using a large running stitch. Pull the thread to gather the edges loosely into a small pouch.
3. Stuff the pouch lightly with fiberfill. Work and manipulate the pouch by flattening and distributing the fiberfill, while at the same time tightening the stitches until you have a gently rounded orange puff. Tuck the edges under the bottom of the puff, far enough for the stitches to be out of sight. Tie and cut off the excess thread.

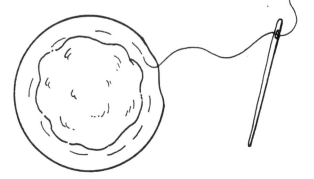

4. Cut four claws and five legs (page 61) from orange felt.

5. Glue or stitch two claws together, leaving the flat end open. If stitching, cut small wedges around the curves and then turn the material inside out. Glue or stitch the other two claws together in the same way.

6. Stuff the ends of the claws lightly with fiberfill. Use a pencil to help push the fiberfill through the narrow opening.
7. Glue the claws to the underside of the body puff.

8. Glue a leg to the backside of each glove finger, with the pointed ends of the legs at the fingertips and the wide ends extending up and overlapping at the center glove back.

12. Repeat Steps 1-11 using the second garden glove.

9. Glue the body puff to the center glove back, with the claws extending out over the knuckles toward the fingertips.
10. Cut a mouth (page 61) from red felt and glue the mouth to the center front of the body puff.
11. Glue black button eyes slightly above the mouth on either side.

The Briny Deep

PUPPETS, POEMS, & SONGS © 1993 Fearon Teacher Aids

Crabs A-Walking
(Tune: "Are You Sleeping?")

Spoken:
When I go down to the seashore,
What do you think I see?
(Raise both crab glove puppets out
of the box and rest your fingertips
on the front edge of the box.)

Sung:
Crabs a-walking, crabs a-walking.
(Walk the crabs from side to side
along the box front by wiggling your
fingers.)

After me, after me.
Little crabs a-walking,
Little crabs a-walking,
After me, after me.

Spoken:
When I go down to the seashore,
What do you think I see?

Crabs A-Walking continued

PUPPETS, POEMS, & SONGS © 1993 Fearon Teacher Aids

Sung:
Crabs a-running, crabs a-running.
(Run the crabs from side to side
along the box front and sing the
song faster.)
After me, after me.
Little crabs a-running,
Little crabs a-running,
After me, after me.

Spoken:
When I go down to the seashore,
What do you think I see?

Sung:
Crabs a-hopping, crabs a-hopping.
(Hop the crabs from side to side
along the box front.)

Continue the song, adding verses
for crabs a-swimming (open and
close your fingers) and crabs a-
whirling (roll your hands over and
over each other). Invite children to
sing along and make the appropriate gestures with you.

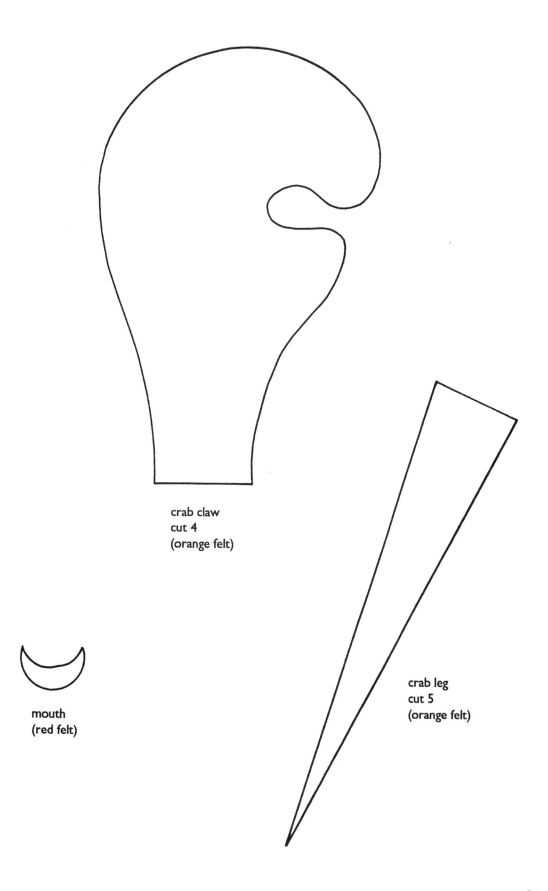

crab claw
cut 4
(orange felt)

crab leg
cut 5
(orange felt)

mouth
(red felt)

The Briny Deep

BOOK CORNER

Allen, Pamela. *Who Sank the Boat?* New York, NY: Coward-McCann, 1982.

Anderson, Lena. *Stina.* New York, NY: Greenwillow Books, 1989.

Carle, Eric. *A House for Hermit Crab.* Natick, ME: Picture Book Studio, 1987.

Conover, Chris. *The Wizard's Daughter.* Boston, MA: Little, Brown, 1984.

Hill, Eric. *Spot Goes to the Beach.* New York, NY: G.P. Putnam's Sons, 1985.

Kalan, Robert. *Blue Sea.* New York, NY: Greenwillow Books, 1979.

Kani, Saru. *The Monkey and the Crab.* Union City, CA: Heian, 1985.

Knutson, Barbara. *Why the Crab Has No Head.* Minneapolis, MN: Carolrhoda, 1987.

Lionni, Leo. *Fish Is Fish.* New York, NY: Pantheon, 1970.

Lionni, Leo. *Swimmy.* New York, NY: Pantheon, 1963.

McCloskey, Robert. *Burt Dow, Deep-Water Man.* New York, NY: Viking, 1963.

Russo, Susan. *The Ice Cream Ocean.* New York, NY: Lothrop, Lee & Shepard, 1984.

Tallon, Robert. *Fish Story.* New York, NY: Holt, Rinehart and Winston, 1977.

Turska, Krystyna. *Tamara and the Sea Witch.* New York, NY: Parents' Magazine Press, 1971.

Waber, Bernard. *I Was All Thumbs.* Boston, MA: Houghton Mifflin, 1975.

COUNTRY CRITTERS

1. Make the box according to the instructions provided on page 16.
2. Cover the outside of the box with beige or gold felt.

COUNTRY CRITTERS

LITTLE BO-PEEP

MATERIALS

- patterns (page 66)
- garden glove
- felt scraps
  black
  pink
  skin-tone
- pom-poms
  1 gold or yellow (1 $^1/_2$") (3.9 cm)
  3 white ($^1/_2$") (1.3 cm)
  1 white (1") (2.5 cm)
  2 white (1 $^1/_2$") (3.9 cm)
  1 black ($^1/_2$") (1.3 cm)
  2 black ($^3/_4$") (1.9 cm)
- 6 half-rounds (3 mm)
- pipe cleaner
- ribbon
  pink satin ribbon (6") (15.2 cm)
  calico (#9)
- miniature straw hat
- pink embroidery floss

Little Bo-Peep

1. Glue a 1 $^1/_2$-inch (3.9 cm) gold or yellow pom-pom to the fingernail side of a glove index fingertip.
2. Make a child's face, dress, arms, and hands (patterns on page 66) according to the instructions provided on pages 19 and 20.
3. Form a crook in one end of a pipe cleaner.
4. Tie a pink satin ribbon in a bow at the bottom of the pipe cleaner crook.
5. Glue the crook under one of Bo-Peep's arms and hands so it looks like she is holding it.
6. Glue a miniature straw hat to Bo-Peep's head.

Sheep

1. Glue a 1 $^1/_2$-inch (3.9 cm) white pom-pom to the second and ring fingers. Glue a $^3/_4$-inch (1.9 cm) black pom-pom to the center of both white pom-poms for noses.
2. Glue a 1-inch (2.5 cm) white pom-pom to the little finger. Glue a $^1/_2$-inch (1.3 cm) black pom-pom to the center of the white pom-pom.
3. Cut four large outer ears and two small outer ears (page 66) from black felt.
4. Cut four large inner ears and two small inner ears (page 66) from pink felt.
5. Glue the inner ears to the outer ears. Glue the assembled ears to the sides of the three pom-poms heads.
6. Glue two half-rounds to each sheep's face above the black nose pom-pom for the eyes.
7. Glue curving threads of pink embroidery floss to the front of each black nose pom-pom. (Cut the threads longer than you need. Draw the curved lines on the pom-poms with glue and lay the embroidery threads into position. Cut off the excess thread after the glue is dry.)

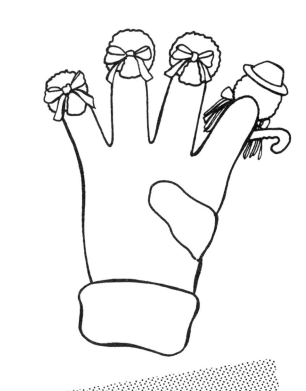

8. For sheep tails, trim three white $^{1}/_{2}$-inch (1.3 cm) pom-poms into triangular shapes and glue them to the palm side of the three glove fingers that have sheep faces on them. The narrow ends of the triangles should be pointing up.

9. Glue a small bow to the top of each tail.

POEM

PUPPETS, POEMS, & SONGS © 1993 Fearon Teacher Aids

Little Bo-Peep

Little Bo-Peep has lost her sheep
(Hold up your index finger.)
And doesn't know where to find them.
Leave them alone
And they will come home
(Raise the sheep.)
Wagging their tails behind them.
(Turn your hand to show the tails and wiggle your fingers.)

Little Bo-Peep, she loves her sheep
(Hold up Bo-Peep only.)
And says she'll never bind them.
Even though they roam,
She knows they'll come home
(Raise the sheep.)
Wagging their tails behind them.
(Turn your hand to show the tails and wiggle your fingers.)

child's face
(skin-tone felt)

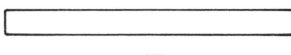

arm
cut 2

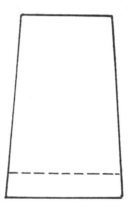

dress
(adjust length as desired)

child's hand
cut 2
(skin-tone felt)

small outer ear
cut 2
(black felt)

small inner ear
cut 2
(pink felt)

large outer ear
cut 4
(black felt)

large inner ear
cut 4
(pink felt)

BABY DUCKLINGS

MATERIALS

- beak and feet patterns (page 69)
- garden glove
- orange felt (3" x 6") (7.6 cm x 15.2 cm)
- pom-poms
  4 yellow (1") (2.5 cm)
  4 yellow (1 1/2") (3.9 cm)
  1 white (1 1/2") (3.9 cm)
  1 white (2") (5.0 cm)
- half-rounds
  8 (3 mm)
  2 (6 mm)
- white and yellow feathers

Baby Ducklings

1. Glue a 1-inch (2.5 cm) yellow pom-pom to the fingernail side of each glove fingertip. Glue nothing to the thumb.
2. Glue a 1 1/2-inch (3.9 cm) yellow pom-pom beneath each 1-inch (2.5 cm) pom-pom.
3. Glue each pair of pom-poms together.
4. Cut four duckling beaks (page 69) from orange felt. Fold the beaks where indicated by the dotted line. Glue the folds to the center of each pom-pom face.
5. Cut eight duckling feet (page 69) from orange felt. Glue the feet to the bottom of each 1 1/2-inch (3.9 cm) pom-pom body. Allow the toes to extend forward slightly in front of the pom-poms.
6. Glue two half-rounds (3 mm) to each duckling face above the beak for the eyes.

Mother Duck

1. Glue a 1 1/2-inch (3.9 cm) white pom-pom to the glove thumb tip.
2. Glue a 2-inch (5.0 cm) white pom-pom beneath it.
3. Glue the two pom-poms together.
4. Cut a mother's beak (page 69) from orange felt. Fold the beak where indicated by the dotted line. Glue the fold to the center of the pom-pom face.
5. Glue two half-rounds (6 mm) above the beak for the eyes.
6. Cut two mother duck feet (page 69) from orange felt and glue the feet to the bottom of the 2-inch (5.0 cm) pom-pom.
7. Glue small white and yellow feathers to each body.

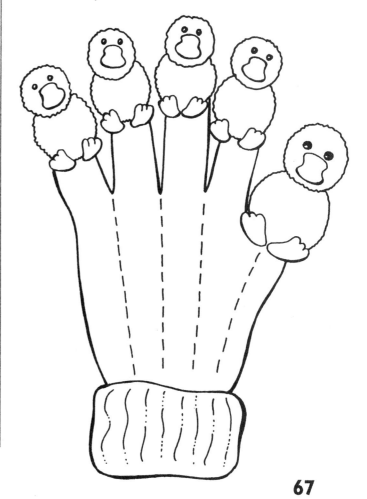

PUPPETS, POEMS, & SONGS © 1993 Fearon Teacher Aids

POEM

Baby Ducklings

One baby duckling,
(Hold up your gloved index finger.)
He's brand new.
Here comes another one.
(Hold up the remaining fingers in succession.)
That makes two.
Two baby ducklings,
Fuzzy as can be.

Wait, here's another.
That makes three.
Three baby ducklings waddling
'cross the floor.
They meet their little brother.
That makes four.
Four baby ducklings.
Watch how they dive.
At last here comes their mother.
(Hold up your thumb.)
That makes five.

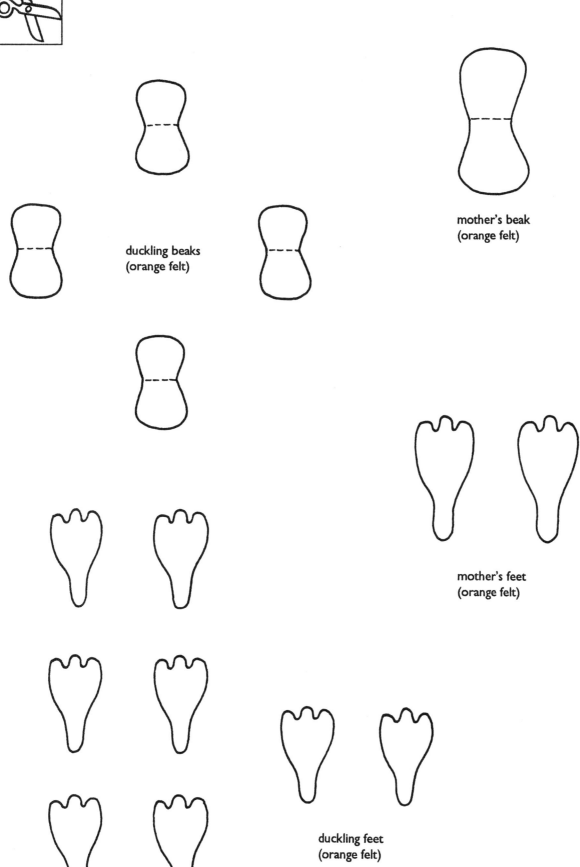

mother's beak
(orange felt)

duckling beaks
(orange felt)

mother's feet
(orange felt)

duckling feet
(orange felt)

BINGO

MATERIALS

- patterns (page 72)
- garden glove
- felt
  red (2" x 7") (5.0 cm x 17.7 cm)
  white (3" x 7") (7.6 cm x 17.7 cm)
  beige (4" x 5") (10.2 cm x 12.7 cm)
  brown (4" x 5") (10.2 cm x 12.7 cm)
- pom-poms
- 5 brown (1 $^1/_2$") (3.9 cm)
- 5 beige ($^3/_4$") (1.9 cm)
- 10 brown crystal animal eyes (9 mm)
- 5 animal noses (10 mm)
- 5 squares of Velcro ($^1/_2$") (1.3 cm)

Bingo Glove Puppet

1. Cut the letter patterns (page 72) from red felt.
2. Cut five background rectangle patterns (page 72) from white felt.
3. Glue the looped side of a Velcro square to each background rectangle where indicated by the dotted lines.
4. Glue each red felt letter to the lower front side of a background rectangle.
5. Glue a 1 $^1/_2$-inch (3.9 cm) brown pom-pom to the fingernail side of each glove fingertip, including the thumb.
6. Glue $^3/_4$-inch (1.9 cm) beige pom-poms to the lower center front of each brown pom-pom.
7. Cut five muzzles (page 72) from beige felt, ten ears (page 72) from brown felt, and five tongues (page 72) from red felt.

8. Glue the muzzles to the dog faces with the long center parts going straight up the center of the larger pom-poms and the flaps coming down on both sides of the smaller pom-poms. Cover the seams where they join together.

9. Glue two eyes to each large pom-pom on each side of the muzzle.
10. Glue a nose to the center top of each smaller pom-pom (with the stem under the front edge of the felt muzzle). If animal noses are not available, glue a black pom-pom (5 mm) or a half-round (6 mm) in the same place.
11. Glue the ears to the top sides of the head pom-poms.
12. Glue a tongue to the bottom of each beige pom-pom.
13. Directly below each dog head, glue the hooked side of a Velcro square. Let the glue dry thoroughly.

14. Velcro the letter squares to the glove fingers so they spell the word "BINGO."

PUPPETS, POEMS, & SONGS © 1993 Fearon Teacher Aids

SONG

BINGO

(Invite the children to sing the song along with you.)
There was a farmer who had a dog
(Hold up the gloved hand.)
And Bingo was his name-oh.
B-I-N-G-O, B-I-N-G-O, B-I-N-G-O
(Wiggle each finger as the letter is named.)
And Bingo was his name-oh.
*(Remove the letter "B." Explain to children that if they don't see a letter, they clap their hands once instead of singing the letter name. Repeat the song.
Remove the letter "I." Repeat the song and remind children to clap once for each missing letter.
Remove the letter "N" and repeat the song.
Remove the letter "G" and repeat the song.
Remove the letter "O" and repeat the song with all claps.)*

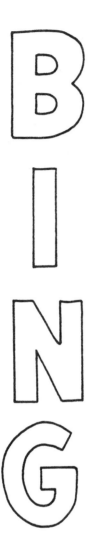

ear
cut 10
(brown felt)

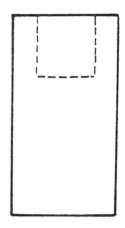

background rectangle
cut 5
(white felt)

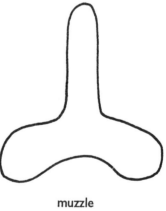

muzzle
cut 5
(beige felt)

tongue
cut 5
(red felt)

letters
(red felt)

PUPPETS, POEMS, & SONGS © 1993 Fearon Teacher Aids

LITTLE BOY BLUE

MATERIALS

- patterns (pages 75-77)
- interfacing (12" x 24") (30.5 cm x 61 cm)
- posterboard (12" x 24") (30.5 cm x 61 cm)
- black permanent marker
- crayons
- 2 plastic straws

Haystack, Sheep, and Cow Stick Puppets

1. Using a black marker, trace the sheep (page 75), cow (page 75), and outer and inner haystack figures (pages 76 and 77) onto interfacing.
2. Color and glue the figures to posterboard, then cut the figures out.
3. Tape a folded posterboard flap to the back of the inner haystack.

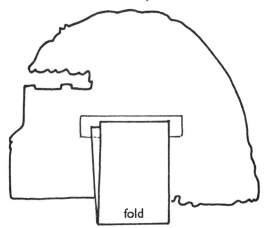

fold

4. Tape straws to the backs of the sheep and cow.
5. Place the outer haystack over the inner haystack and fold the tabs down to hold

the outer haystack in place. The two pieces should be placed as a single unit on the box front, with the flap on the back of the inner haystack supporting the entire assembly.

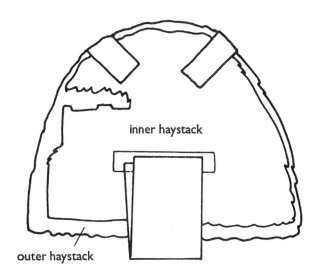

inner haystack

outer haystack

front of presentation box

PUPPETS, POEMS, & SONGS © 1993 Fearon Teacher Aids

POEM

Little Boy Blue

Little Boy Blue, come blow your horn.
(Place the haystack assembly on the box front.)
The sheep's in the meadow
(Place the sheep.)
The cow's in the corn.
(Place the cow.)
Where is the little boy who looks after the sheep?

He's under the haystack, fast asleep.
(Lift off the top haystack.)
Will you wake him?
No, not I.
For if I do,
He'll surely cry.
(Pretend to cry.)

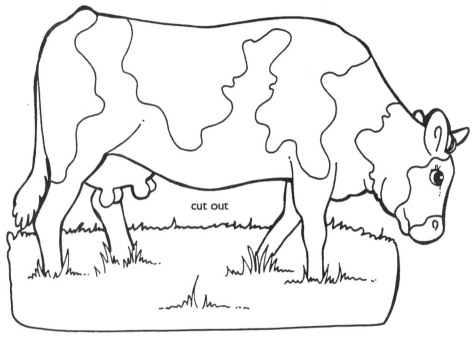

cut out

cow
(interfacing)

cut out

sheep
(interfacing)

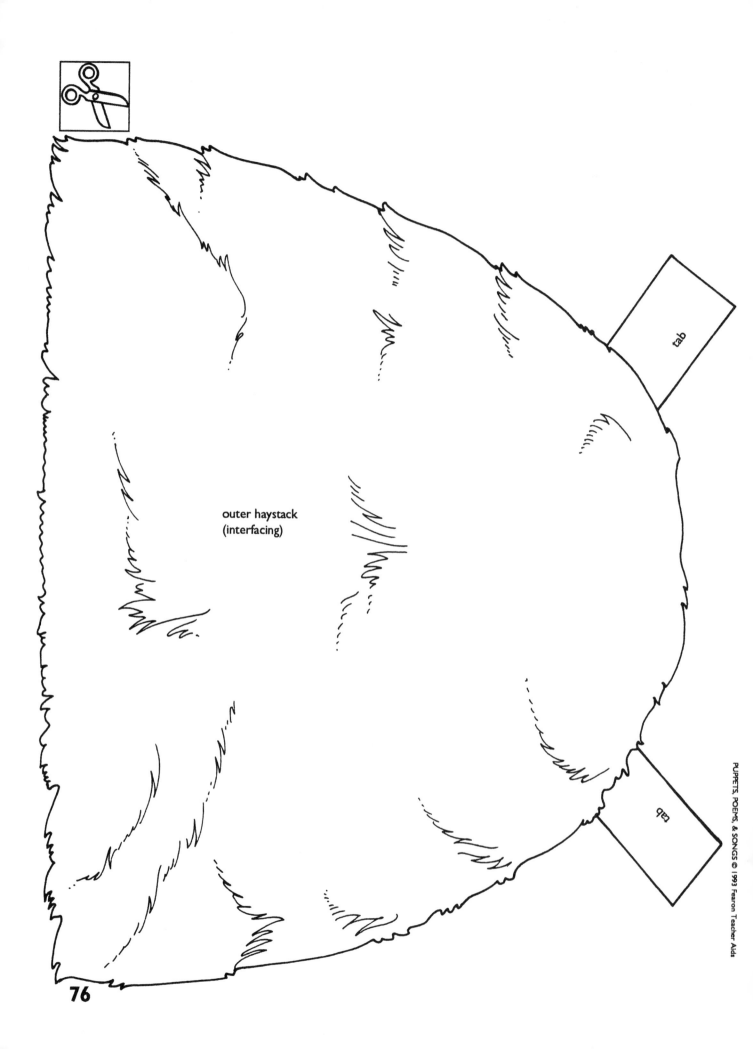

outer haystack
(interfacing)

tab

tab

PUPPETS, POEMS, & SONGS © 1993 Fearon Teacher Aids

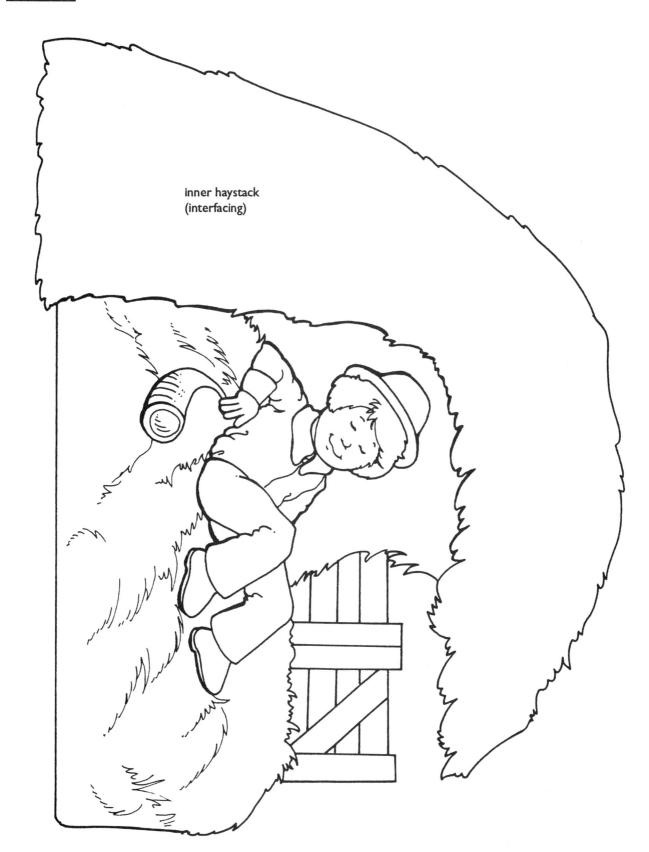

inner haystack
(interfacing)

BAA, BAA, BLACK SHEEP
MATERIALS

- patterns (pages 81 and 82)
- garden glove
- felt scraps
  black
  skin-tone
  pink
  gray
  assorted colors
- pom-poms
  1 black (1") (2.5 cm)
  1 black (2") (5.0 cm)
  3 any color ($^1/_2$") (1.3 cm)
  1 white (1 $^1/_2$") (3.9 cm)
  1 gray (1 $^1/_2$") (3.9 cm)
  1 brown (1 $^1/_2$") (3.9 cm)
- 2 wiggly eyes (8 mm)
- pink embroidery floss
- miniature props, such as a hat and wire glasses
- yarn
- small bell
- ribbon

Sheep

1. Glue a 2-inch (5.0 cm) black pom-pom to the fingernail side of a glove index finger.
2. Glue a 1-inch (2.5 cm) black pom-pom to the front of the larger pom-pom just below the center. Trim the top and bottom of the smaller pom-pom so that it is more oval than round.
3. Glue two curving strands of pink embroidery floss to the center front of the smaller pom-pom. (Cut the threads longer than you need. Draw the curved lines on the pom-poms with glue and lay the embroidery threads into position. Cut off the excess thread after the glue is dry.)
4. Cut two outer ears (page 82) from black felt and two inner ears from pink felt. Glue the inner ears to the outer ears.
5. Glue the assembled ears to the sheep head pom-pom.
6. Glue wiggly eyes above the nose pom-pom.
7. Tie a ribbon bow to a bell and glue the bell to the glove under the sheep's chin.

Master

1. Glue a 1 $^1/_2$-inch (3.9 cm) gray pom-pom to the fingernail side of the second glove finger.
2. Make the man's face, clothes, arms, and hands (see patterns on pages 81 and 82) according to the instructions provided on pages 20 and 21.
3. Cut a small top hat from black felt and glue the hat to the man's head.

Dame

1. Glue a 1 1/2-inch (3.9 cm) white pom-pom to the fingernail side of the glove ring finger.
2. Make the woman's face, clothes, arms, and hands (see patterns on page 81) according to the instructions provided on pages 19 and 20.
3. Add hat, wire glasses, and other miniature props as desired.

Little Boy

1. Glue a 1 1/2-inch (3.9 cm) brown pom-pom to the fingernail side of the glove little finger.
2. Make the boy's face, clothes, arms, and hands (see patterns on pages 81 and 82) according to instructions provided on pages 20 and 21.

Country Critters

Bags

1. Cut three bags (page 82) from gray felt.
2. Glue a $\frac{1}{2}$-inch (1.3 cm) pom-pom (any color) to the back of each bag.
3. Glue around the back edges of each bag, then glue the bags to the center back of the glove.
4. Glue a yarn bow across the narrow neck of each bag.

Baa, Baa, Black Sheep

Baa, baa, black sheep,
Have you any wool?
(Hold up the gloved index finger.)
Yes, sir, yes, sir
(Nod.)
Three bags full.
(Point to the bags on the glove.)
One for my master,
(Raise the second finger.)
One for my dame,

(Raise the ring finger.)
One for the little boy who lives down the lane.
(Raise the little finger.)
Baa, baa, black sheep,
Have you any wool?
Yes, sir, yes, sir, three bags full.
(Point to the bags on the glove.)

child's head

woman's head

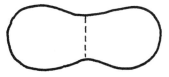

man's head

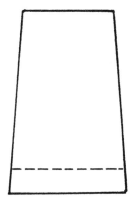

dress
(adjust length as desired)

child's hand
cut 2
(skin-tone felt)

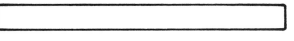

arm
cut 6

adult's hand
cut 4
(skin-tone felt)

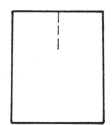

child's shirt

sheep's inner ear
cut 2
(pink felt)

wool bag
cut 3
(gray felt)

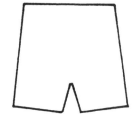

child's pants

child's vest

sheep's outer ear
cut 2
(black felt)

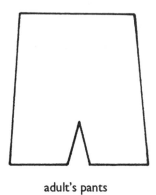

adult's pants

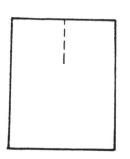

adult's shirt

82

THE HUNGRY PIGS

MATERIALS

- patterns (page 85)
- pair of garden gloves
- pink felt (3" x 8") (7.6 cm x 20.3 cm)
- pom-poms
  8 pink (1 1/2") (3.9 cm)
  8 pink (1/4") (6 mm)
  2 pink (2") (5.0 cm)
  2 pink (1/2") (1.3 cm)
- 16 black rocaille beads
- half-rounds
  4 (3 mm)
  16 (4 mm)
  4 (6 mm)

Piggies

1. Glue a 1 1/2-inch (3.9 cm) pink pom-pom to the fingernail side of each glove fingertip.
2. Glue a 1/4-inch (6 mm) pink pom-pom to the center of each small pig's face.
3. Cut eight small snouts (page 85) from pink felt and glue one to the front of each 1/4-inch (6 mm) pink pom-pom.
4. Glue two black rocaille beads to each small pig's snout for nostrils.
5. Glue two half-rounds (4 mm) to each small pig's face, just above the snout, for eyes.
6. Cut sixteen small ears (page 85) from pink felt.
7. Overlap the flaps on either side of the notch in each ear and glue the lower parts of the flaps together to give the ears shape and depth.

8. Glue two ears to each pig toward the front of each head pom-pom so that the ears flop forward.

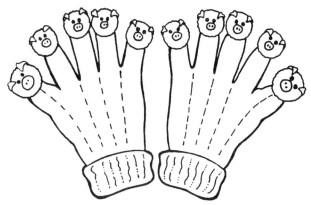

Mama and Papa Pig

1. Glue a 2-inch (5.0 cm) pink pom-pom to each glove thumb.
2. Glue a 1/2-inch (1.3 cm) pink pom-pom to the center of each large pig's face.
3. Cut two large snouts (page 85) from pink felt and glue one to the front of each 1/2-inch (1.3 cm) pink pom-pom.
4. Glue two half-rounds (3 mm) to each large pig's snout for nostrils.
5. Glue two half-rounds (6 mm) to each large pig's face, just above the snout, for eyes.
6. Cut four large ears (page 85) from pink felt.
7. Overlap the flaps on either side of the notch in each ear and glue the lower part of the flaps together to give the ears shape and depth.
8. Glue two ears to each pig toward the front of each head pom-pom so that the ears flop forward.

Country Critters

PUPPETS, POEMS, & SONGS © 1993 Fearon Teacher Aids

POEM

The Hungry Pigs

Four little pigs by the barnyard gate
(Hold up four fingers of your right hand.)
Said, "Where's our supper? It's getting very late!"
(Wiggle your fingers as though the pigs are talking.)
Four more little pigs came to join the others,

(Hold up four fingers of your left hand.)
And that made eight little piggie brothers.
Then Mama Pig
(Reveal the right thumb.)
And Papa Pig
(Reveal the left thumb.)
Said, "Come, children, come.

The Hungry Pigs continued

(Wiggle the thumbs.)
Come get your supper, yum, yum, yum."
So ten pigs ran to get their meal,
(Run your hands back and forth.)
And you should have heard those piggies squeal!
Then ten pink pigs curled up in a heap,

(Curl up your hands and bring them together.)
They all closed their eyes and went to sleep.
(Close your eyes.)

PUPPETS, POEMS, & SONGS © 1993 Fearon Teacher Aids

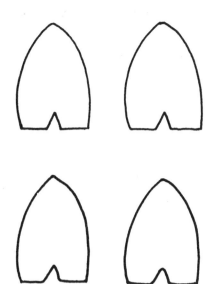

large pig ears
(pink felt)

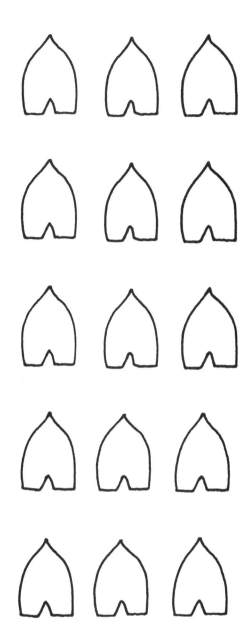

large pig snouts
(pink felt)

small pig snouts
(pink felt)

small pig ears
(pink felt)

HIGGLEDY, PIGGLEDY, MY BLACK HEN

MATERIALS

- patterns (pages 88 and 89)
- interfacing (10" x 12") (25.4 cm x 30.5 cm)
- posterboard (10" x 14") (25.4 cm x 35.5 cm)
- black permanent marker
- crayons
- straw
- book tape

Nest, Lady and Gentleman, and Hen Stick Puppets

1. Using a black marker, trace the hen, nest, and large egg (page 88) and lady and gentleman figures (page 89) onto interfacing.
2. Color and glue the figures to posterboard and then cut the figures out.
3. Tape a folded posterboard flap to the back of the nest.

4. Tape a straw to the back of the large egg.
5. Tape the top of the large egg to the back of the hen, about halfway up the hen's body. This will enable you to fit the hen down over the front side of the nest with the large egg hidden.
6. Before reading the first line of the poem, place the assembled nest piece on the front edge of the box stage so that the posterboard flap taped to the back of the nest is down in the box slot. The bottom edge of the nest should overlap the front edge of the box. This will allow the nest to support the entire assembly. Do not put the large egg, or the straw taped to the back of it, down inside the box slot. Leave them free so you can hold the straw and push the hen up to reveal the large egg.

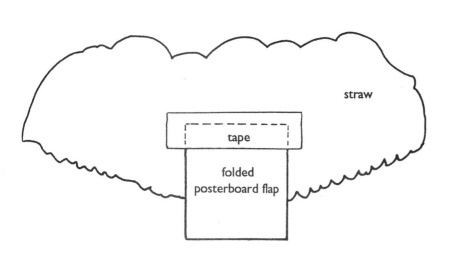

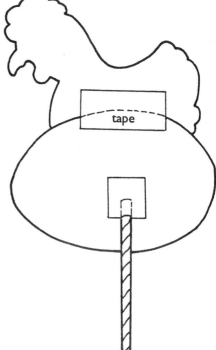

front view

back view

POEM

Higgledy, Piggledy, My Black Hen

Higgledy, piggledy, my black hen
(Place the nest assembly.)
She lays eggs for a lady and
gentleman.
Lady and gentleman come every
day
(Place the lady and gentleman.)
To see what my black hen doth lay.

Higgledy, piggledy, my black hen,
She lays eggs for a lady and
gentleman.
Sometimes nine, and sometimes
ten!
(Let out a loud squawk, then push
the hen up.)
Higgledy, piggledy, my black hen.

nest
(interfacing)

hen
(interfacing)

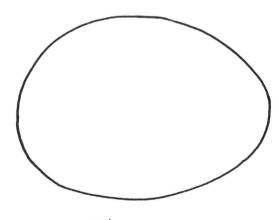

large egg
(interfacing)

PUPPETS, POEMS, & SONGS © 1993 Fearon Teacher Aids

lady and gentleman
(interfacing)

OLD MACDONALD
MATERIALS

- patterns (pages 96 and 97)
- pair of garden gloves
- felt scraps
  skin-tone
  orange
  pink
  brown
  beige
  black
  gold
  red
- pom-poms
  1 yellow (1") (2.5 cm)
  1 pink (¹/₄") (6 mm)
  1 pink (1 ¹/₂") (3.9 cm)
  2 white (1 ¹/₂") (3.9 cm)
  3 white (¹/₄") (6 mm)
  1 gold (1") (2.5 cm)
  1 gold (1 ¹/₂") (3.9 cm)
  1 beige (³/₄") (1.9 cm)
  2 brown (1 ¹/₂") (3.9 cm)
  1 brown (2") (5.0 cm)
  1 black (³/₄") (1.9 cm)
  1 black (1 ¹/₂") (3.9 cm)
  2 gray (1 ¹/₂") (3.9 cm)
- half-rounds
  2 (4 mm)
  8 (3 mm)
  2 (6 mm)
  2 rocaille beads
  4 crystal eyes (9 mm)
  2 cat eyes (9 mm)
- animal nose (10 mm)
- fabric scraps
  denim
  gingham or bandanna-print
- embroidery floss
  black
  pink
  cream
- fine monofilament fishing line
- grosgrain ribbon (¹/₈-inch (3 mm) wide)
- miniature straw farmer's hat
- miniature cow bell (¹/₄ inch (6 mm) or ¹/₂ inch (1.3 cm), gold or copper finish)

Old MacDonald

1. Glue a 1 ¹/₂-inch (3.9 cm) gray pom-pom to the right-hand glove index finger.
2. Make a man's face, shirt, hands, and arms (see patterns on page 96) according to the instructions provided on pages 20 and 21.
3. Cut a pair of overalls (page 96) from denim fabric.
4. Glue the overalls over the shirt.
5. Cut a scarf (page 96) from gingham or bandanna-print fabric and tie it around Old MacDonald's neck.
6. Glue a miniature straw farmer's hat to the top of his head.

Chick

1. Glue a 1-inch (2.5 cm) yellow pom-pom to the second finger of the right-hand glove.
2. Cut a chick beak (page 96) from orange felt. Fold the beak in half where indicated by the dotted line.
3. Glue the folded end of the beak into the pom-pom fibers in the center of the chick's face.
4. Glue two half-rounds (3 mm) above the beak for the eyes.

Pig

1. Glue a 1 1/2-inch (3.9 cm) pink pom-pom to the ring finger of the right-hand glove.
2. Glue a 1/4-inch (6 mm) pink pom-pom to the center of the face.
3. Cut a snout (page 96) from pink felt and glue the snout to the front of the 1/4-inch (6 mm) pink pom-pom.
4. Glue two black rocaille beads to the snout for nostrils.
5. Glue two half-rounds (4 mm) to the face just above the snout for eyes.
6. Cut two ears (page 96) from pink felt.
7. Overlap the flaps on either side of the notch in each ear and glue the flaps together to give the ear shape and depth.
8. Glue the ears to the pig toward the front of the head pom-pom so that the ears flop forward.

Duck

1. Glue a 1 1/2-inch (3.9 cm) white pom-pom to the little finger of the right-hand glove.
2. Cut a beak (page 96) from orange felt.
3. Fold the beak where indicated by the dotted line. Glue the fold to the center of the pom-pom face.
4. Glue two half-rounds (6 mm) above the beak for eyes.

Cow

1. Glue a 2-inch (5.0 cm) brown pom-pom to the index finger of the left-hand glove.
2. Glue a 1 1/2-inch (3.9 cm) brown pom-pom to the front of the larger pom-pom, just below the center.
3. Cut two outer ears (page 97) from brown felt.
4. Cut two inner ears (page 97), one nose (page 97), and two horns (page 97) from beige felt. Cut one tongue (page 97) from pink felt.

5. Glue the felt nose to the center front of the smaller pom-pom with the top edge of the nose along the top edge of the smaller pom-pom.

6. Glue crystal eyes to the larger pom-pom, just above the smaller pom-pom.

7. Glue the inner ears to the outer ears. Glue the assembled ears to the sides of the head pom-pom.

8. Glue the horns just above the ears.

9. Trim short threads from black embroidery floss and glue them to the top of the head between the horns as fringe.

10. Glue a miniature bell under the cow's face.

Sheep

1. Glue a 1 ¹/₂-inch (3.9 cm) white pom-pom to the second finger of the left-hand glove.

2. Glue a ³/₄-inch (1.9 cm) black pom-pom to the center of the white pom-pom for the nose.

3. Cut two outer ears (page 97) from black felt and two inner ears (page 97) from pink felt.

4. Glue the inner ears to the outer ears. Glue the ears to the sides of the head pom-pom.

5. Glue two half-rounds (3 mm) to the face above the black nose pom-pom.

6. Glue curving threads of pink embroidery floss to the front of the black nose pom-pom. (Cut the threads longer than you need. Draw curved lines on the pom-poms with glue and then place the embroidery threads into position. Cut off the excess thread after the glue is dry.)

Horse

1. Glue a 1 ¹/₂-inch (3.9 cm) gold pom-pom to the ring finger of the left-hand glove.

2. Glue a 1-inch (2.5 cm) gold pom-pom to the lower center front of the larger pom-pom.

3. Glue two half-rounds (3 mm) in place for eyes.

4. Cut two outer ears (page 97) from gold felt and two inner ears (page 97) from beige felt.

5. Glue the inner ears to the outer ears. Pinch the ears together along the dotted line and glue in place. Glue the ears fairly close together on top of the horse's head.

6. Cut strands of cream embroidery floss and glue to the center top of the head, between the ears, coming down onto the center forehead.

7. Glue a strip of ¹/₈-inch (3 mm) grosgrain ribbon around the nose pom-pom where

it joins the head pom-pom. Glue additional strips of ribbon at an angle on each side of the face, from the nose pom-pom to behind the ears, to create a halter.

Turkey

1. Glue a 1 1/2-inch (3.9 cm) gray pom-pom to the little finger of the left-hand glove.
2. Cut a turkey beak (page 97) from gold felt and fold the beak in half where indicated by the dotted line. Glue the turkey beak to the center front of the head pom-pom.
3. Cut a wattle (page 97) from red felt. Drape the wattle over the beak and glue in place.
4. Add two half-rounds (3 mm) for eyes.

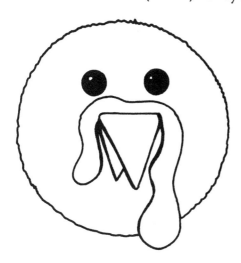

Dog

1. Glue a 1 1/2-inch (3.9 cm) brown pom-pom to either glove thumb.
2. Glue a 3/4-inch (1.9 cm) beige pom-pom to the lower center front of the brown pom-pom.
3. Cut a muzzle (page 97) from beige felt, two ears (page 97) from brown felt, and a tongue (page 97) from pink felt.
4. Glue the muzzle to the dog's face with the long center part going straight up the center of the larger pom-pom and the flaps coming down on both sides of the smaller pom-pom. Be sure to cover the seam where the pom-poms join together.
5. Glue two crystal eyes (9 mm) to the large pom-pom on each side of the muzzle.
6. Glue an animal nose to the center top of the smaller pom-pom (with the stem under the front edge of the felt muzzle). If animal noses are not available, glue a 5 mm black pom-pom or a 6 mm half-round in the same place.
7. Glue the ears to the top sides of the head pom-pom.
8. Glue the tongue on the bottom of the beige pom-pom.

Country Critters

Cat

1. Glue a 1 ¹/₂-inch (3.9 cm) black pom-pom to the other glove thumb.
2. Glue three ¹/₄-inch (6 mm) white pom-poms in a triangle in the lower center of the large pom-pom. Glue the small pom-poms to each other as well as to the larger pom-pom.
3. Cut two outer ears (page 97) from black felt and a nose (page 97) and two inner ears (page 97) from pink felt.
4. Glue the nose to the center top of the ¹/₄-inch (6 mm) pom-poms with the point of the nose coming forward and down over the space between the two side-by-side pom-poms.
5. Glue the inner ears to the outer ears. Glue the assembled ears to the top of the cat's head.

6. Glue two cat eyes (9mm) just above the nose pom-poms.
7. Glue lengths of very fine monofilament fishing line to the two nose pom-poms for whiskers.

POEM

PUPPETS, POEMS, & SONGS © 1993 Fearon Teacher Aids

Old MacDonald

Old MacDonald had a farm,
E-I, E-I, Oh!
(Hold up Old MacDonald.)
And on this farm he had some
chicks, E-I, E-I, Oh!
(Hold up the chick.)
With a chick, chick here, and a
chick, chick there,
Here a chick, there a chick, every-
where a chick, chick.

Old MacDonald had a farm,
E-I, E-I, Oh!
Old MacDonald had a farm,
E-I, E-I, Oh!
And on this farm he had some
pigs, E-I, E-I, Oh!
(Hold up the pig.)
With an oink, oink here, and an
oink, oink there,
Here an oink, there an oink, every-
where an oink, oink.
Old MacDonald had a farm,
E-I, E-I, Oh!

Old MacDonald continued

Other Verses:
And on this farm he had some
ducks . . . with a quack, quack
here . . .
(Hold up the duck.)
And on this farm he had some
cows . . . with a moo, moo here . . .
(Hold up the cow.)
And on this farm he had some
sheep . . . with a baa, baa here . . .
(Hold up the sheep.)
And on this farm he had some
horses . . . with a neigh, neigh
here . . .
(Hold up the horse.)

And on this farm he had some
turkeys . . . with a gobble, gobble
here . . .
(Hold up the turkey.)
And on this farm he had some
dogs . . . with a woof, woof here . . .
(Hold up the dog.)
And on this farm he had some
cats . . . with a meow, meow
here . . .
(Hold up the cat.)

PUPPETS, POEMS, & SONGS © 1993 Fearon Teacher Aids

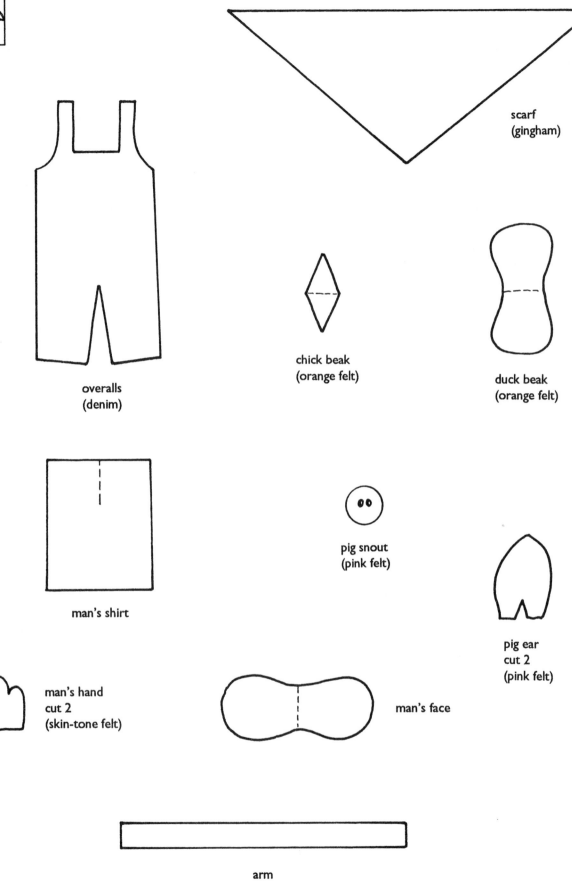

scarf
(gingham)

overalls
(denim)

chick beak
(orange felt)

duck beak
(orange felt)

man's shirt

pig snout
(pink felt)

pig ear
cut 2
(pink felt)

man's hand
cut 2
(skin-tone felt)

man's face

arm
cut 2

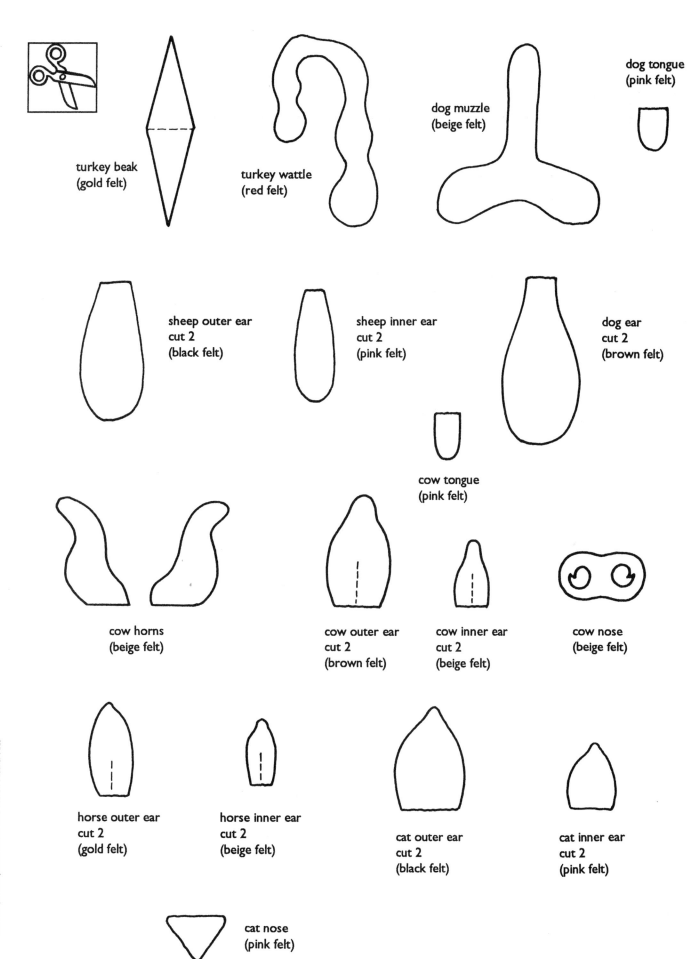

turkey beak
(gold felt)

turkey wattle
(red felt)

dog muzzle
(beige felt)

dog tongue
(pink felt)

sheep outer ear
cut 2
(black felt)

sheep inner ear
cut 2
(pink felt)

dog ear
cut 2
(brown felt)

cow tongue
(pink felt)

cow horns
(beige felt)

cow outer ear
cut 2
(brown felt)

cow inner ear
cut 2
(beige felt)

cow nose
(beige felt)

horse outer ear
cut 2
(gold felt)

horse inner ear
cut 2
(beige felt)

cat outer ear
cut 2
(black felt)

cat inner ear
cut 2
(pink felt)

cat nose
(pink felt)

97

Country Critters

BOOK CORNER

Alborough, Jez. *The Grass Is Always Greener.* New York, NY: Dial, 1987.

Allen, Pamela. *Fancy That!* New York, NY: Orchard, 1987.

Barrett, Judith. *Old MacDonald Had an Apartment House.* New York, NY: Atheneum, 1969.

Brown, Margaret Wise. *Big Red Barn.* New York, NY: Harper & Row, 1989.

Ginsburg, Mirra. *Good Morning, Chick.* New York, NY: Greenwillow Books, 1980.

Goldin, Augusta. *Ducks Don't Get Wet.* New York, NY: Harper & Row, 1989.

Heine, Helme. *The Most Wonderful Egg in the World.* New York, NY: Atheneum, 1983.

Heller, Ruth. *Chickens Aren't the Only Ones.* New York, NY: Grosset & Dunlap, 1981.

Holl, Adelaide. *The Rain Puddle.* New York, NY: Lothrop, Lee & Shepard, 1965.

Hutchins, Pat. *Rosie's Walk.* New York, NY: Macmillan, 1968.

Inkpen, Mick. *If I Had a Sheep.* Boston, MA: Little, Brown, 1988.

Kitamura, Satoshi. *When Sheep Cannot Sleep.* New York, NY: Farrar, Strauss & Giroux, 1986.

Krause, Ute. *Pig Surprise.* New York, NY: Dial, 1989.

Lobel, Arnold. *A Treeful of Pigs.* New York, NY: Greenwillow Books, 1979.

Lyon, David. *The Runaway Duck.* New York, NY: Lothrop, Lee & Shepard, 1985.

McCloskey, Robert. *Make Way for Ducklings.* New York, NY: Viking Press, 1941.

Nodset, Joan. *Who Took the Farmer's Hat?* New York, NY: Harper & Row, 1963.

Preston, Edna. *Squawk to the Moon, Little Goose.* New York, NY: Viking, 1974.

Roy, Ron. *Three Ducks Went Wandering.* New York, NY: Seabury, 1979.

Spier, Peter. *The Fox Went Out on a Chilly Night.* New York, NY: Doubleday, 1976.

CREEPY CRAWLIES

1. Make the box according to the instructions provided on page 16.
2. Finish the box by following the additional instructions provided on page 100.

CREEPY CRAWLIES PRESENTATION BOX

1. Place your spread fingertips about 3 inches (7.6 cm) from the top of the box on the long side of the box, opposite the side with the posterboard flap.

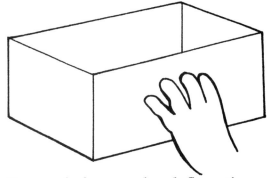

2. Draw a circle around each fingertip.
3. Cut out the circles through both thicknesses of cardboard (box side and flap) with an X-acto knife. The holes should be large enough for your fingers to fit through easily.
4. Make a second posterboard flap and hold it against the side of the box with the cut-out holes.
5. Trace the holes onto the posterboard and cut through both thicknesses before taping the posterboard inside the box.

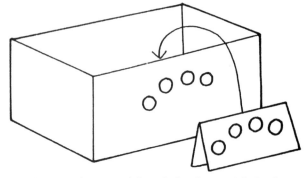

6. Cover the outside of the box with **beige** or gold felt.

7. Trace the holes onto the felt and cut the traced holes out. Be sure to glue the felt securely around the hole edges to prevent the felt from fraying and stretching.
8. Cut the fingers off a brown garden glove about $1/2$ inch (1.3 cm) below where the fingers are attached to the palm.

9. Poke the glove fingers through the box holes from the inside to the outside, so the fingers hang down on the outside of the box.
10. Glue or tape the raw edges of the glove inside the box.

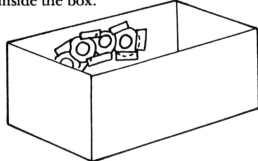

11. Have the plain side of the box facing the audience for all the poems in this section, except for "Hepzibah Rose." When presenting "Hepzibah Rose," turn the box around so the side with the glove fingers is facing the audience.

ROLY-POLY CATERPILLAR

MATERIALS

- pattern (page 102)
- garden glove
- felt scraps (any color)
- pom-poms
  2 green ($^1/_2$") (1.3 cm)
  4 green ($^3/_4$") (1.9 cm)
  4 pink, orange, or yellow (2") (5.0 cm)
  2 brown ($^1/_2$") (1.3 cm)
  3 brown ($^3/_4$") (1.9 cm)
- 2 eyes (3 mm)
- 2 half-rounds (3 mm)
- 2 real flower stamens
- decorating trims, such as sequins, glitter, ribbon, or paint

Caterpillar

1. Glue four $^3/_4$-inch (1.9 cm) green pom-poms along the length of the palm side of the glove index finger. (This is an exception to the general rule for making glove puppets.)
2. Glue a $^1/_2$-inch (1.3 cm) green pom-pom to each end of the row.
3. Glue all the pom-poms to each other.

4. Glue a 2-inch (5.0 cm) pink, orange, or yellow pom-pom to the top of each $^3/_4$-inch (1.9 cm) pom-pom.
5. Glue two eyes (3 mm) to the $^1/_2$-inch (1.3 cm) pom-pom at the fingertip end of the caterpillar.

Butterfly

1. Cut one butterfly (page 102) from any color felt and glue it to the center back of the glove.
2. Starting at the top of the butterfly, glue three $^3/_4$-inch (1.9 cm) brown pom-poms in a row down the center of the felt wings. Glue a $^1/_2$-inch (1.3 cm) brown pom-pom to the bottom of the row.
3. Glue all the pom-poms to each other and glue a $^1/_2$-inch (1.3 cm) brown pom-pom to the top $^3/_4$-inch (1.9 cm) pom-pom so it extends beyond the felt body for the butterfly's head.
4. Glue two half-rounds (3 mm) to the top $^1/_2$-inch (1.3 cm) brown pom-pom.
5. Glue two flower stamens to the top of the head for antennae.
6. Decorate the wings with sequins, glitter, ribbon, or shiny paint.

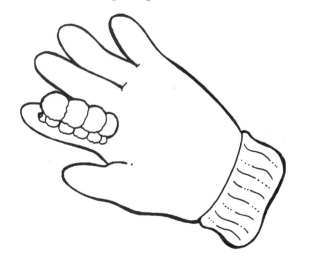

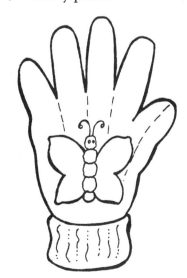

Creepy Crawlies

POEM

PUPPETS, POEMS, & SONGS © 1993 Fearon Teacher Aids

Roly-Poly Caterpillar

Roly-poly caterpillar,
(Hold up the index finger of the
caterpillar side of the glove.)
Crawling all around.
Roly-poly caterpillar,
High above the ground.
Go inside your little house,
(Bend your fingers down into a
fist and cover the caterpillar
completely with your thumb.
Yawn.)

Cover up your little head.
Have yourself a little snooze
In your silky little bed.
Roly-poly caterpillar,
Wake up by and by.
(Swiftly turn the glove around,
with the caterpillar still hidden, to
reveal the butterfly.)
Now you have two lovely wings,
You are a butterfly.

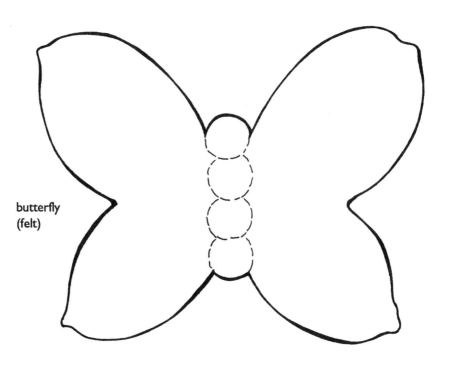

butterfly
(felt)

PUPPETS, POEMS, & SONGS © 1993 Fearon Teacher Aids

SNAKE-IN-THE-GRASS

MATERIALS

- patterns (page 105)
- felt
  yellow (4" x 9") (10.2 cm x 22.9 cm)
  red scrap
  green (5" x 5") (12.7 cm x 12.7 cm)
- 2 wiggly eyes (12 mm)
- posterboard (5" x 7") (12.7 cm x 17.7 cm)
- book tape
- straw

Snake

1. Cut one snake head (page 105) from yellow felt and one snake head from posterboard. Glue the two together.
2. Cut a tongue (page 105) from red felt. Glue the tongue in place on the felt head.
3. Glue two wiggly eyes to the felt head.
4. Cut a snake body (page 105) from yellow felt.
5. Glue the head to the body where indicated by the dotted lines.

Grass

1. Cut one grass block (page 105) from green felt and one grass block from posterboard. Cut the posterboard block 1/2 inch (1.3 cm) shorter than the felt block as indicated by the dotted line. Glue the two together, with the bottom and sides even and the extra felt sticking up above the top of the posterboard block.
2. Fringe the 1/2-inch (1.3 cm) felt strip by cutting slits every 1/4 inch (6 mm).

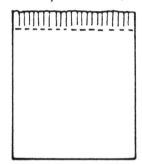

3. Glue the snake body to the top back side of the grass block where indicated by the dotted line.
4. Make a manipulator for the back of the snake's head according to the instructions provided on page 25.

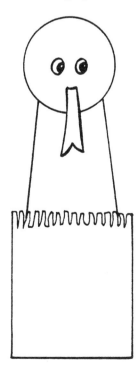

POEM

Snake-in-the-Grass

See the grass in the garden?
(Hold up the grass.)
See it shiver and shake?
(Shake the grass.)
What makes it do that?
A bright yellow snake!
(Pop up the snake.)
Hissssssss.

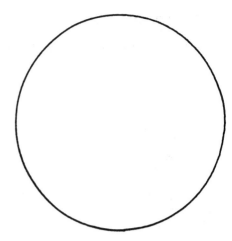

snake head
cut 2
(yellow felt/posterboard)

grass block
cut 2
(green felt/posterboard)

snake tongue
(red felt)

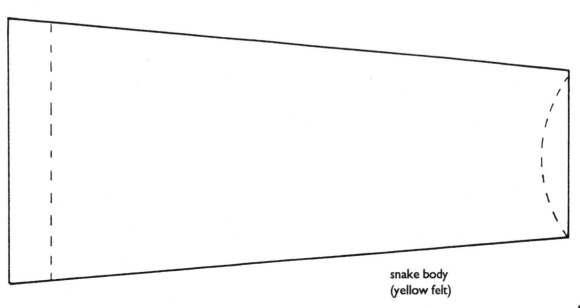

snake body
(yellow felt)

Creepy Crawlies

ONE LITTLE SPIDER

MATERIALS

- garden glove
- 5 beige pom-poms (1 ¹/₂") (3.9 cm)
- 10 eyes (6 mm)
- thin black yarn
- wooden dowel (¹/₄" x 8") (6 mm x 20.3 cm)
- broom straw

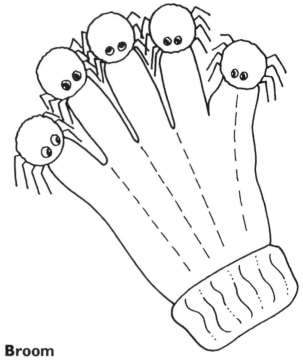

Spider Glove Puppet

1. Cut four 4-inch (10.2 cm) strands of thin black yarn for each glove finger.
2. Arrange each set of four strands, crossing the strands in the middle, so they look like eight spider legs. Glue the center of the legs to the fingernail side of each glove fingertip.

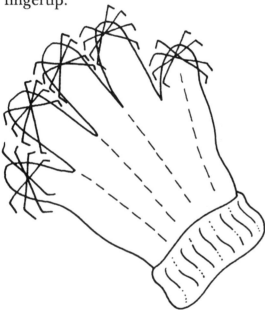

3. Center and glue a 1 ¹/₂-inch (3.9 cm) beige pom-pom to each fingertip over the yarn legs.
4. Glue two eyes near the top of each pom-pom.

Broom

Using yarn, tie a clump of broom straw around one end of a dowel.

Bring the broom up out of the puppet box on the next-to-last line of the poem.

106

PUPPETS, POEMS, & SONGS © 1993 Fearon Teacher Aids

POEM

One Little Spider

One little spider, feeling rather blue.
(Hold up one gloved finger at
a time.)
Along comes another one.
Now there are two.
Two little spiders crawling up
a tree.
Along comes another one.
Now there are three.
Three little spiders spinning by the
door.
Along comes another one.
Now there are four.

Four little spiders glad to be alive.
Here comes another one.
Now there are five.
Five little spiders, all their webs
are spun.
Whack! goes the broom,
(Whack at the spider glove with
the broom.)
Now there are none.
(Run the spiders behind your
back.)

HOW DOES A CATERPILLAR GO?

MATERIALS

- 6 pom-poms, any color (2") (5.0 cm)
- 2 eyes (12 mm)
- 2 bamboo skewers
- decorating trim, such as yarn, chenille stems, beads, or sequins

Caterpillar

1. Using plenty of glue, stick five of the pom-poms together in a row.
2. Insert the pointed ends of two bamboo skewers between the last and next-to-last pom-poms at each end so that the skewers extend out from the row of pom-poms in a perpendicular line.
3. When the glue is dry, cut off the ends of the skewers so that they extend only 4 inches (10.2 cm) beyond the pom-pom row.

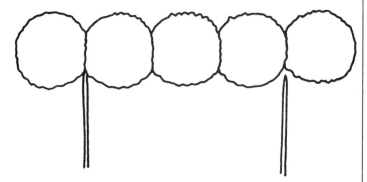

4. Position the caterpillar so that the ends of the skewers are pointing toward you. With the skewers in this position, glue the sixth pom-pom on top of either of the end pom-poms to make the caterpillar's head.

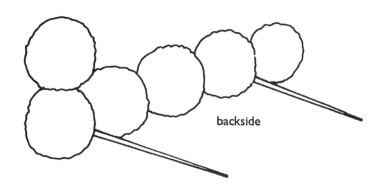

backside

5. Glue two eyes on the head. The caterpillar's face should be looking in the opposite direction of the skewers sticking out.
6. Add other facial features, such as a pom-pom or sequin nose, crescent sequin eyebrows, yarn mouth, and chenille-stem antennae with beads or sequins.
7. You might also want to add pom-pom spots, yarn fringe, or feather hair. Let your imagination go wild!

SONG

PUPPETS, POEMS, & SONGS © 1993 Fearon Teacher Aids

How Does a Caterpillar Go?

How does a caterpillar go?
(Place the caterpillar on the front
edge of the box.)
Can anyone tell me?
Does anyone know?
How does a caterpillar go
On his leaf so green?

Chorus: (Tune: "The Worms Go In")
Creepy, creep
(Manipulate the caterpillar
forward in a hunching crawl.)

Creepy, creep
Creepy, creepity, creepy, creep.
Creepy, creep
Creepy, creep
Creepy, creepity, creep.
(Repeat the chorus with the
children joining you and creeping
their fingers up their arms as you
move the caterpillar back across
the box front.)

I SEE A LITTLE SPOTTED SHELL

MATERIALS

- patterns (page 112)
- green felt (9" x 12") (22.9 cm x 30.5 cm)
- 2 wiggly eyes (10 mm)
- posterboard (5" x 7") (12.7 cm x 17.7 cm)
- book tape
- straw

Turtle Puppet

1. Cut one turtle head (page 112) from green felt and one turtle head from posterboard. Glue the two together.
2. Cut one turtle shell (page 112) from green felt and one turtle shell from posterboard. Glue the two together.
3. Cut four feet (page 112), two eyelids (page 112), a tail (page 112), and a body pattern (page 112) from green felt.
4. Glue the feet and the tail to the backside of the shell where indicated by the dotted lines.
5. Glue the head to the body and the body to the front of the shell where indicated by the dotted lines.
6. Glue two wiggly eyes to the turtle head. Glue the eyelids over the top half of the eyes.
7. Make a manipulator for the back of the turtle's head according to the instructions provided on page 25.

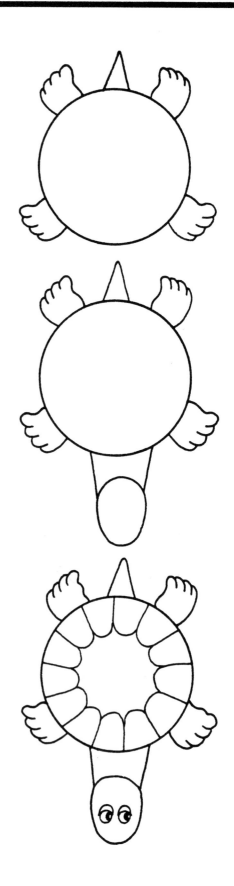

POEM

I See a Little Spotted Shell

I see a little spotted shell
(Hold up the turtle shell.)
I see a tail and feet.
At last, here comes a little head.
(Pop up the turtle.)
My turtle is complete.

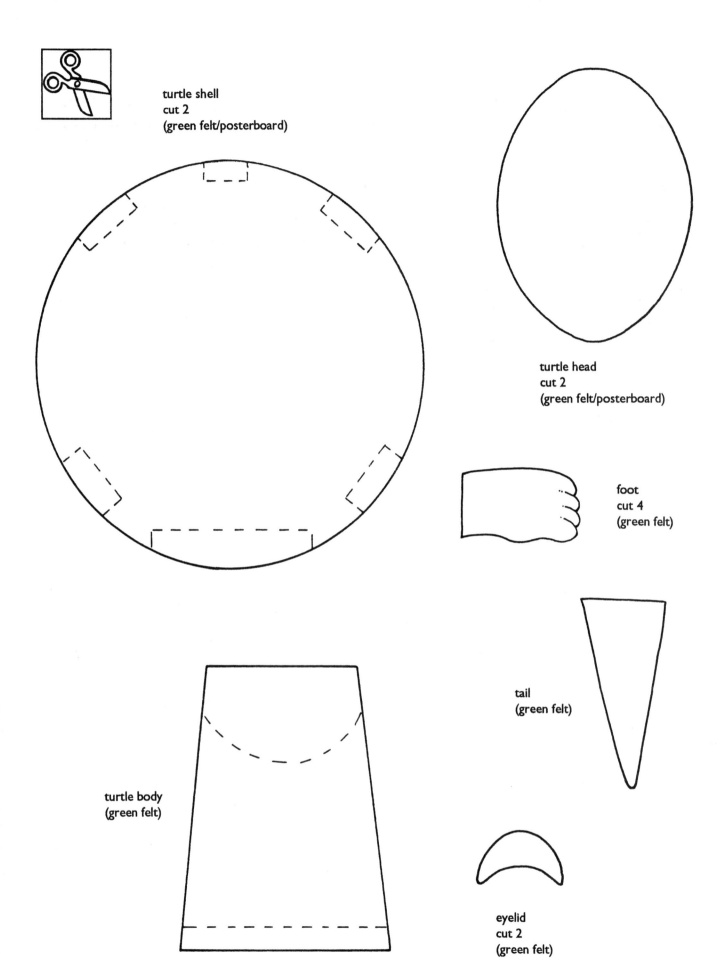

turtle shell
cut 2
(green felt/posterboard)

turtle head
cut 2
(green felt/posterboard)

foot
cut 4
(green felt)

tail
(green felt)

turtle body
(green felt)

eyelid
cut 2
(green felt)

112

THE BUGABOO IS CREEPING

MATERIALS

- pattern (page 115)
- pair of garden gloves
- felt (9" x 12") (22.9 cm x 30.5 cm)
- plastic cup (9 oz) (282 mL)
- decorating trim, such as pom-poms, sequins, felt scraps, chenille stems, bottle caps, and golf tees

Bugaboo Glove Puppet

1. Trace around the bottom of a plastic cup on any color felt.
2. Cut out the felt circle and glue it to the outside bottom of the cup.
3. Cut out a cup cover (page 115) and cover the cup with the same color felt according to the instructions provided on page 25.
4. Put on a pair of gloves and stick your thumbs into the cup opposite each other. Pull outward against the sides of the cup. Note each thumb's position on the cup, then remove the gloves. Glue the glove thumbs to the cup in the exact positions where they were when your hands were in the gloves.

5. Make a face on the felt circle on the bottom of the cup using pom-poms and other decorating trims. Glue odd felt shapes or sequin spots to the bugaboo body. Make bumpy chenille antennae, a bottle-cap nose, or golf tee eyes. Let your imagination run wild!

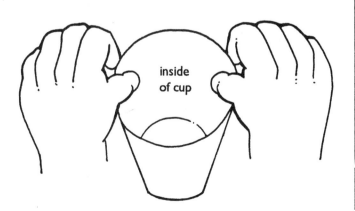

Creepy Crawlies

POEM

PUPPETS, POEMS, & SONGS © 1993 Fearon Teacher Aids

The Bugaboo Is Creeping

The bugaboo is creeping.
(Creep the fingers of both gloved
hands up onto the box front
edge.)
Shhhhhh! Shhhhhh!
The bugaboo is creeping.
(Bring your thumbs and the cup
body slowly up out of the box.)

Shhhhhh! Shhhhhh!
He doesn't make a sound,
(Creep the bugaboo from side to
side along the box edge.)
As he crawls across the ground.
The bugaboo is creeping.
Shhhhhhh! Shhhhhhh!

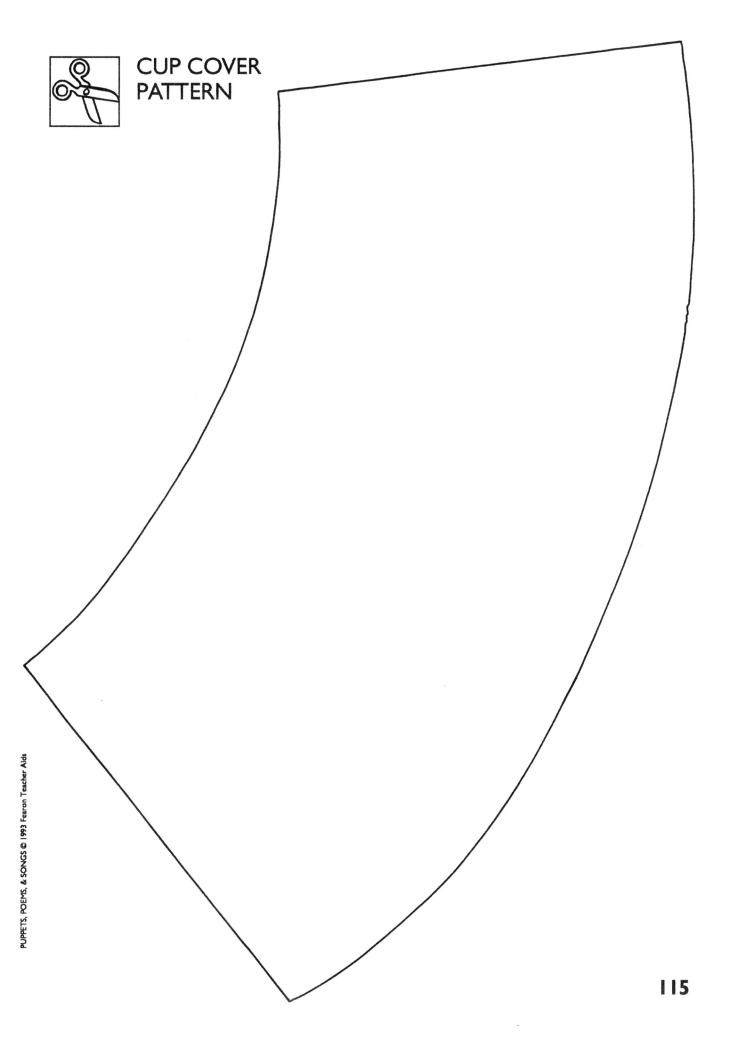

CUP COVER
PATTERN

HEPZIBAH ROSE

MATERIALS

- patterns (page 118)
- 2 paper plates (7") (17.7 cm)
- felt scraps
  green
  red
- paint (red and green)
- wiggly eyes
  2 (15 mm)
  2 (20 mm)
- dowel (^{1}/4-inch thick) (6 mm)
- felt, vinyl, or plush fabric (5" x 6") (12.7 cm x 15.2 cm)
- book tape
- fiberfill
- decorating trim, such as fake eyelashes, pom-poms, rickrack, sequins, and yarn

Rose Paper-Plate Puppet

1. Paint the bottoms of two paper plates red. Let the paint dry thoroughly.
2. Decorate the center of the red side of one plate with wiggly eyes (20 mm), fake eyelashes, pom-poms, feathers, rickrack, and sequins to make a flower's face.
3. Paint a wooden dowel green. Let the paint dry thoroughly.
4. Cut two leaves (page 118) from green felt.
5. Tape one end of the dowel to the unpainted side of the paper plate without the face.
6. Place the face plate on top of the back plate, sandwiching the dowel in between. Staple or glue the plates together around the edges. If you use scalloped plates, be sure to match the scallops.
7. Glue the two leaves to the dowel just below the plates.

Worm

1. Cut two worms (page 118) from felt, vinyl, or plush fabric.
2. Stitch on the dotted line and turn the material inside out. Or, you may use hot glue around the dotted line instead.
3. Cut a mouth (page 118) from red felt and glue in place.
4. Glue a wiggly eye (15 mm) to each side of the worm's face.
5. Decorate with yarn hair, sequins, pompoms, or feathers as desired.
6. Stuff the worm's head lightly with fiberfill.

7. To manipulate the worm, slip your index finger inside and wiggle.

PUPPETS, POEMS, & SONGS © 1993 Fearon Teacher Aids

POEM

Hepzibah Rose

(Turn the puppet box around so the side with the holes faces the audience. Stick your gloved fingers out the holes.)
One day a flower named Hepzibah Rose
(Place the flower's stem down into the slot between the two middle glove fingers that are sticking out through the root holes.)
Said, "Something is wiggling and tickling my toes!"

(Wiggle your gloved fingers and squirm your shoulders.)
She laughed and she giggled,
Then quite suddenly,
Up popped a worm
Who said, "Whoops!
Pardon me!"
(Raise the index finger of the ungloved hand with the worm. Wiggle the worm as if speaking.)

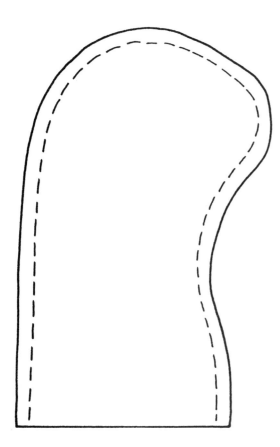

worm
cut 2
(felt, vinyl, or plush fabric)

mouth
(red felt)

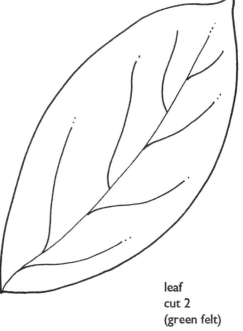

leaf
cut 2
(green felt)

PUPPETS, POEMS, & SONGS © 1993 Fearon Teacher Aids

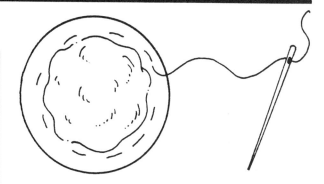

ITSY BITSY SPIDER

MATERIALS

- patterns (pages 122 and 123)
- garden glove
- felt
  brown or black (8" x 8") (20.3 cm x 20.3 cm)
  red scrap
- 2 eyes (20 mm)
- interfacing (9" x 12") (22.9 cm x 30.5 cm)
- posterboard (9" x 12") (22.9 cm x 30.5 cm)
- black permanent marker
- carpet or buttonhole thread and needle
- black pom-pom ($^1/_4$") (6 mm)
- crayons
- 2 plastic straws
- book tape
- tinsel
- fiberfill

Spider Glove Puppet

1. Cut an 8-inch (20.3 cm) circle from black or brown felt.
2. With carpet or buttonhole thread, stitch around the circle $^1/_2$ inch (1.3 cm) from the outer edge, using a large running stitch. Pull the thread to gather the edges loosely into a small pouch.
3. Stuff the pouch lightly with fiberfill. Work and manipulate the pouch by flattening and distributing the fiberfill, while at the same time tightening the stitches until you have a full and rounded puff. Tuck the edges under the bottom of the puff, enough to hide the stitches. Tie the thread and then cut off the excess.

4. Glue the filled puff to the back of a glove.
5. Glue two eyes to the front of the puff.
6. Add a pom-pom nose and a felt mouth.

Sun Stick Puppet

1. Using a black marker, trace a sun (page 122) onto interfacing.
2. Color and glue the sun to posterboard, then cut the sun out.
3. Tape a straw to the back of the sun.

119

Creepy Crawlies

Rain Wand

1. Cut a narrow piece of book tape and put it aside temporarily by sticking one edge of the tape to the edge of a table.
2. Drape a small bundle (20 to 30 strands) of tinsel over your right index finger.

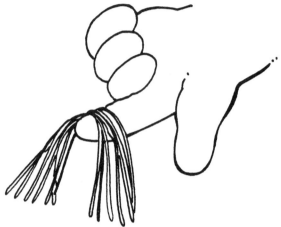

3. Grasp the bundle with your left thumb and index finger just below the right index finger. Pull the resulting loop off your right index finger.

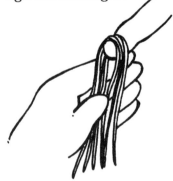

4. Insert the tip of a straw into the loop of tinsel just far enough to grasp it, along with the looped clump of tinsel, between your left thumb and forefinger.

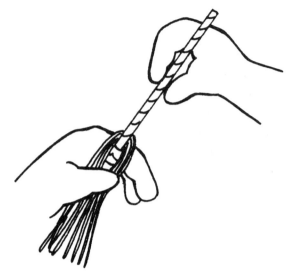

5. Tape the folded tinsel to the tip of the straw using the book tape you set aside earlier. Start the tape at the end and roll it tightly around the straw. Be sure to catch all of the tinsel.

6. The tinsel will hang down from one tip of the straw. Hold the straw by the other end and flutter downward to make rain.

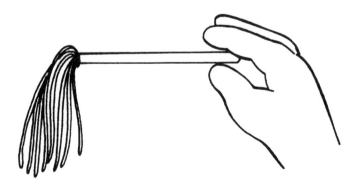

Waterspout Stick Puppet

1. Using a black marker, trace a waterspout (page 123) onto interfacing.
2. Color and glue the waterspout to posterboard, then cut the waterspout out.
3. Tape a folded posterboard flap to the back of the waterspout.

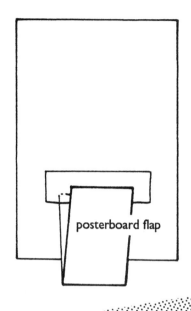

posterboard flap

PUPPETS, POEMS, & SONGS © 1993 Fearon Teacher Aids

SONG

Itsy Bitsy Spider

(Place the waterspout in the front slot before beginning the song.)
Itsy bitsy spider
Went up the waterspout.
(Crawl the spider up out of the box and up the spout.)
Down came the rain
(Flutter the rain wand down.)
And washed the spider out.

(Sweep the spider down beside the box.)
Out came the sun,
(Hold up the sun.)
And dried up all the rain.
(Sway the sun back and forth.)
And the itsy bitsy spider
Went up the spout again.
(Crawl the spider up out of the box and up the spout again.)

sun
(interfacing)

PUPPETS, POEMS, & SONGS © 1993 Fearon Teacher Aids

waterspout
(interfacing)

Extend pattern down to desired length.

Creepy Crawlies

BOOK CORNER

Aardema, Verna. *Why Mosquitoes Buzz in People's Ears.* New York, NY: Dial, 1975.

Asch, Frank. *Turtle Tale.* New York, NY: Dial, 1978.

Barrett. Judi. *A Snake Is Totally Tail.* New York, NY: Atheneum, 1983.

Barton, Byron. *Buzz Buzz Buzz.* New York, NY: Macmillan, 1973.

Carle, Eric. *The Mixed-Up Chameleon.* New York, NY: Crowell, 1984.

Carle, Eric. *The Very Busy Spider.* New York, NY: Philomel, 1989.

Carle, Eric. *The Very Hungry Caterpillar.* New York, NY: Philomel, 1979.

Dugan, William. *The Bug Book.* New York, NY: Golden Press, 1965.

Galdone, Paul. *The Turtle and the Monkey.* New York, NY: Clarion, 1983.

Graham, Margaret Bloy. *Be Nice to Spiders.* New York, NY: Harper & Row, 1967.

Kepes, Juliet. *Lady Bird, Quickly.* Boston, MA: Little, Brown, 1964.

Lionni, Leo. *The Biggest House in the World.* New York, NY: Pantheon, 1968.

Lobel, Arnold. *Grasshopper on the Road.* New York, NY: Harper & Row, 1978.

O'Donnell, Elizabeth Lee. *I Can't Get My Turtle to Move.* New York, NY: Morrow Junior Books, 1989.

O'Neal, Zibby. *Turtle and Snail.* New York, NY: Lippincott, 1979.

Peet, Bill. *The Ant and the Elephant.* Boston, MA: Houghton Mifflin, 1972.

Peet, Bill. *The Gnats of Knotty Pine.* Boston, MA: Houghton Mifflin, 1975.

Seuss, Dr. *Yertle the Turtle.* New York, NY: Random House, 1958.

FAR OUT!

1. Make the box according to the instructions provided on page 16.
2. Cover the outside of the box with navy blue felt.
3. Glue sequin stars and crescent moons to the box front.

Far Out!

STAR LIGHT, STAR BRIGHT
MATERIALS

- pattern (page 127)
- interfacing (6" x 6") (15.2 cm x 15.2 cm)
- posterboard (6" x 6") (15.2 cm x 15.2 cm)
- black permanent marker
- liquid glitter
- crayons
- plastic straw
- book tape

Star Stick Puppet

1. Using a black marker, trace a star (page 127) onto interfacing.

2. Color and glue the star to posterboard. Paint the star with liquid glitter, then cut the star out.
3. Tape a plastic straw to the back of the star.

POEM

Star Light, Star Bright

Star light, star bright
(Hold up the star.)
First star I see tonight.
I wish I may, I wish I might
Have the wish I wish tonight.

star
(interfacing)

Far Out!

TWINKLE, TWINKLE LITTLE STAR

MATERIALS

- pattern (page 129)
- interfacing (6" x 6") (15.2 cm x 15.2 cm)
- posterboard (6" x 6") (15.2 cm x 15.2 cm)
- black permanent marker
- liquid glitter
- crayons
- 2 plastic straws
- book tape

STAR STICK PUPPET

1. Using a black marker, trace two stars (page 129) onto interfacing.
2. Color and glue the stars to posterboard. Paint the stars with liquid glitter, then cut the stars out.

3. Tape a plastic straw to the back of each star.

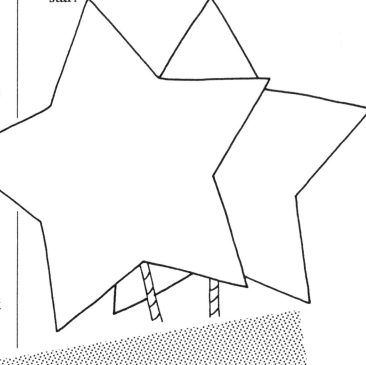

PUPPETS, POEMS, & SONGS © 1993 Fearon Teacher Aids

Twinkle, Twinkle Little Star

Twinkle, twinkle, little star
(Hold up both star puppets.)
How I wonder what you are.
Up above the world so high,
Like a diamond in the sky.
Twinkle, twinkle, little star,
How I wonder what you are.

Twinkle, twinkle through the night
Spreading forth your gentle light.
Little children in the dark
Thank you for your tiny spark.
Twinkle, twinkle, little star
How I wonder what you are.

star
cut 2
(interfacing)

HEY DIDDLE DIDDLE

MATERIALS

- patterns (pages 131 and 132)
- interfacing (11" x 12") (27.9 cm x 30.5 cm)
- posterboard (11" x 12") (27.9 cm x 30.5 cm)
- black permanent marker
- crayons
- 4 plastic straws

Stick Puppets

1. Using a black marker, trace a cat (page 131), cow (page 132), dog (page 132), moon (page 131), and dish and spoon (page 131) onto interfacing.
2. Color and glue the figures to posterboard, then cut the figures out.
3. Tape a straw to the back of each figure.

(Tape the moon below the cow on the same straw.)

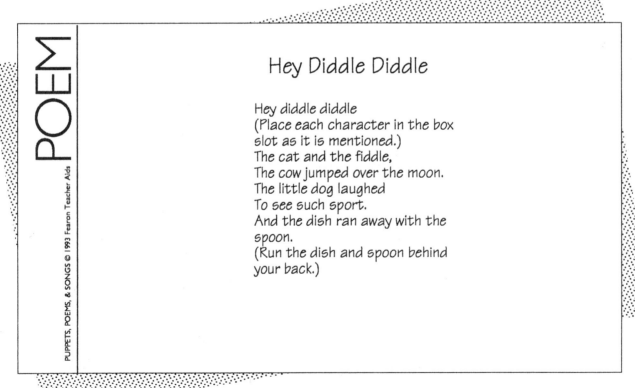

POEM

PUPPETS, POEMS, & SONGS © 1993 Fearon Teacher Aids

Hey Diddle Diddle

Hey diddle diddle
(Place each character in the box slot as it is mentioned.)
The cat and the fiddle,
The cow jumped over the moon.
The little dog laughed
To see such sport.
And the dish ran away with the spoon.
(Run the dish and spoon behind your back.)

THE MAN IN THE MOON

MATERIALS

- patterns (page 135)
- 2 paper plates (9") (22.9 cm)
- felt
  yellow (4" x 4") (10.2 cm x 10.2 cm)
  white (4" x 4") (10.2 cm x 10.2 cm)
- silver paint
- glitter (gold, silver, or violet)
- interfacing (4" x 4") (10.2 cm x 10.2 cm)
- black permanent marker
- crayons
- calico ribbon (#9)
- lace
- paint stick

Moon

1. Paint the bottoms of two paper plates silver. Apply gold, silver, or violet glitter to both plates while they are still wet. Let the paint dry thoroughly.
2. Cut a 3-inch (7.6 cm) square from the center of one of the plates.
3. Cut a 4-inch (10.2 cm) square of yellow felt.
4. Cut two curtains (page 135) from calico ribbon and trim with lace.
5. Glue the curtains to the right and left sides of the 4-inch (10.2 cm) yellow felt square.
6. Position the assembled felt square behind the 3-inch (7.6 cm) opening in the paper-plate moon, so the curtains are partly visible through the opening. Glue or tape the felt square in place on the unpainted side of the moon plate.

Man

1. Using a black marker, trace the man in the moon (page 135) onto interfacing.
2. Color and glue the man to white felt, then cut the man out.
3. Glue the man on the moon opening (on top of the curtained background). Place the man's chin on the bottom of the window opening. The man's hands should curve over the bottom of the window opening.
4. Tape a paint stick to the unpainted side of the solid moon plate.
5. Position the windowed moon so the man is upright when you hold the moon puppet by the stick. Staple the plates together around the rim.

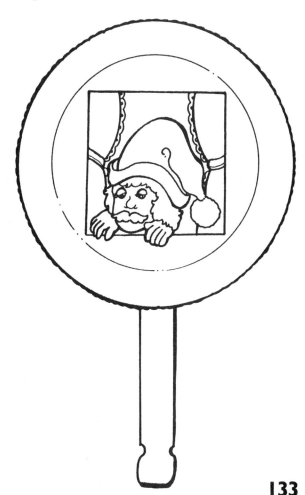

Far Out!

POEM

PUPPETS, POEMS, & SONGS © 1993 Fearon Teacher Aids

The Man in the Moon

The man in the moon
(Hold up the moon puppet.)
Looked out of the moon
(Turn the moon around.)
And this is what he said.
"How sad that when I'm getting up,
Most children go to bed."

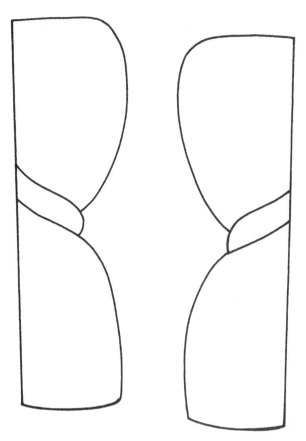

curtains
(calico ribbon)

man in the moon
(interfacing)

Far Out!

HERE'S A LITTLE SPACESHIP

MATERIALS

- patterns (pages 138 and 139)
- felt
  gray (7" x 7") (17.7 cm x 17.7 cm)
  any color (6" x 7") (15.2 cm x 17.7 cm)
- self-adhesive Velcro (¼-inch square)
  (6 mm)
- posterboard (9" x 12") (22.9 cm x
  30.5 cm)
- brad fastener
- book tape
- straw
- decorating trim, such as red sequins,
  beads, chenille stems, or pom-poms

Martian

1. Cut one Martian head (page 139) from
   posterboard and one from any color felt.
   Glue the two heads together.
2. Make features on the Martian head using
   decorating trim, such as chenille stems
   for antennae, and so on. Be creative!
3. Cut the Martian body (page 139) from
   the same color felt as the head.
4. Glue the head to the body.
5. Make a manipulator on the back of the
   Martian's head according to the instructions provided on page 25.

SPACESHIP

1. Cut one spaceship top and one spaceship
   bottom (page 138) from posterboard and
   one top and bottom from gray felt. Glue
   the felt and posterboard pieces together.
2. Poke a hole in each spaceship piece
   where indicated.
3. Stick Velcro pieces on the spaceship
   where indicated. Place the hooked side
   of the Velcro square on the front of the
   spaceship bottom and the looped side of
   the Velcro square on the back of the
   spaceship top.
4. Glue red sequins along the bottom edge
   of the spaceship for lights.
5. Glue the Martian body to the spaceship.
6. Insert the brad fastener through the
   holes in the top and bottom of the spaceship to connect the two pieces.

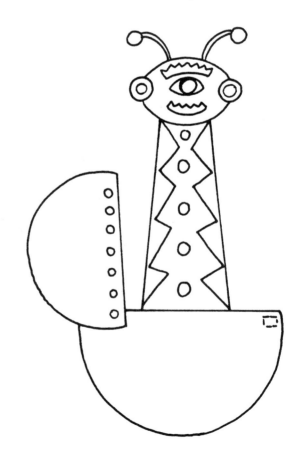

POEM

Here's a Little Spaceship

Here's a little spaceship
(Hold up the spaceship.)
I wonder who's in here.
(Slowly lift the top.)
A friendly little Martian!
(Pop up the Martian.)
Let's welcome him with cheer!

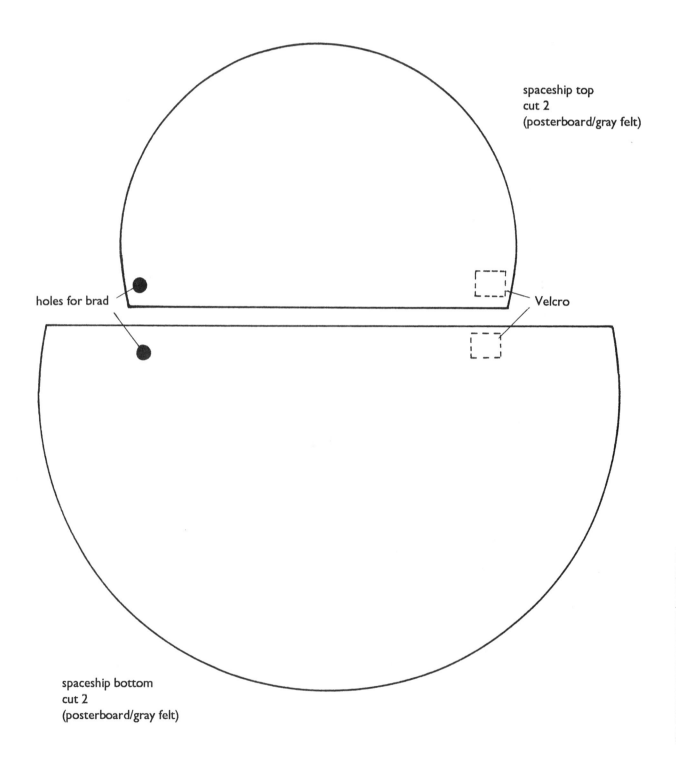

spaceship top
cut 2
(posterboard/gray felt)

holes for brad

Velcro

spaceship bottom
cut 2
(posterboard/gray felt)

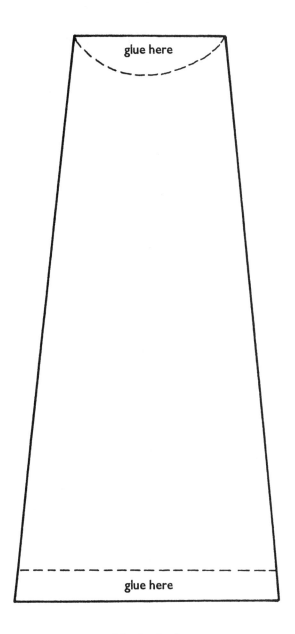

glue here

glue here

Martian body
(felt)

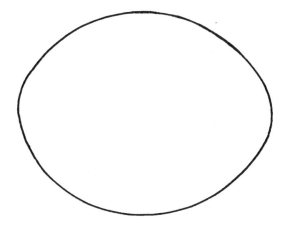

Martian head
cut 2
(posterboard/felt)

Far Out!

ON SATURDAY NIGHT

MATERIALS

- patterns (pages 142 and 143)
- interfacing (10" x 15") (25.4 cm x 38.1 cm)
- posterboard (10" x 15") (25.4 cm x 38.1 cm)
- black permanent marker
- crayons
- wooden dowel ($^1/_4$" x 12") (6 mm x 30.5 cm)
- self-adhesive Velcro ($^1/_4$-inch square) (6 mm)
- bamboo skewer
- fine monofilament fishing line
- Christmas-ornament hook

Moon Stick Puppet, Girl, and Stars

1. Using a black marker, trace a moon (page 143), girl (page 142), and stars (page 142) on interfacing.
2. Color and glue the figures to posterboard, then cut the figures out.
3. Tape a wooden dowel to the back of the moon.
4. Strengthen the girl's leg by gluing a bamboo-skewer splint to the back of the tab, extending the skewer up onto the leg.
5. Stick the hooked side of the Velcro square to the front side of the tab that extends down from the girl's foot. Stick the looped side of the Velcro square to the top of the moon puppet on the back side.

6. Poke holes in the moon and stars where indicated.
7. Tie fishing line through the holes.
8. Tie the loose ends of the fishing line to a small Christmas-ornament hook so the stars hang at different levels.

with a lighter shade of green marker or fabric paint.

2. Glue a 1 ¹/₂-inch (3.9 cm) green pompom between the two nose pieces, with the vein lines on the outside. Secure the pom-pom by gluing all around the edges of both nose pieces.

3. Glue the flat edge of the assembled nose to the center of the cardboard tube just below the eye.

Mouth

1. Cut a mouth (page 148), lip circle (page 148), and tooth (page 148)—each from a different color of felt.

2. Glue the wide part of the tooth to the top of the mouth.

3. Glue the lip circle to the mouth over the tooth at the top and under the tooth at the bottom.

4. Glue the mouth to the front of the cardboard tube below the nose, with the tooth pointing down.

Ears

1. Cut two ears (page 148) from purple felt.

2. Glue one ear to each side of the head beside the eye.

Arms and Hands

1. Cut three 1" x 10" (2.5 cm x 25.4 cm) strips from any color felt for arms.

2. Glue a chenille stem along the center of each arm strip. Fold the strip in half and glue the edges together.

3. Cut six hands (page 148) from any color felt and glue the hands to the ends of the arms.

4. Glue the three arms to the back of the cardboard tube, one below the other. The arms should appear below the facial features in the front. Curve the arms forward towards the front of the tube and glue them in place. You can bend the arms with elbows up, down, or any way you wish.

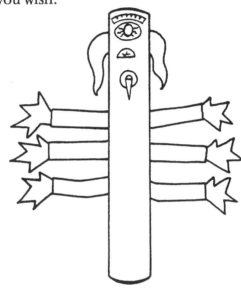

Hair

1. Cut a toilet-tissue tube up the middle and press it flat. Anchor it with something heavy (a stapler or tape dispenser) so you can work with it without it constantly rolling back up on you.

2. Cut several 8-inch (20.3 cm) lengths of yarn, iridescent gift-wrap ribbon, or tinsel.

3. Spread a 1-inch (2.5 cm) strip of glue along the top edge of the flattened toilet-tissue tube.

4. Set the lengths of yarn side by side on the glue with the ends extending out beyond the top edge of the tube. Let the glue dry thoroughly.

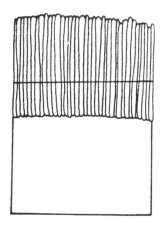

5. Secure the glued ends of the yarn with book tape. Cut the tape longer than the width of the tube so you can fold the tape edges over at each end.

6. Turn the toilet-tissue tube over and repeat the yarn-gluing process on the inside top edge. Let the glue dry thoroughly.

7. Tape the dowel in the center of the inside of the toilet-tissue tube. Roll the tube back up. Overlap the ends slightly so that the tube is smaller than it was originally. Secure the tube in place with a small piece of tape and fit it down inside the cardboard body tube. Adjust the size of the hair tube until it can be moved up and down freely inside the larger body tube by manipulating the dowel.

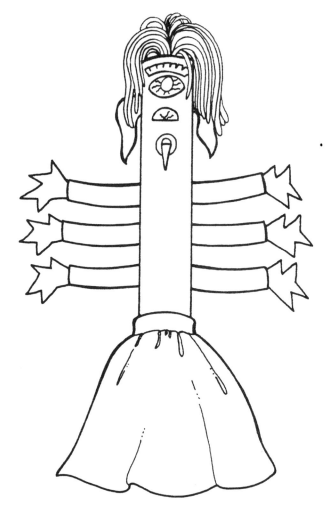

8. When you first bring the space person up out of the box, grab the bottom of the outer tube and the inner dowel in the same hand (behind the skirt), and bring him up with just a little of the hair showing above the top of the head. As you recite the poem, you can take hold of the dowel with the other hand so it can be pushed up at the appropriate time.

POEM

PUPPETS, POEMS, & SONGS © 1993 Fearon Teacher Aids

There Are People in Space?

There are people in space, have you heard?
There are people in space, but don't say a word.
(Hold up finger to lips.)
Just keep it a secret, and don't make a fuss, 'cause they don't exactly . . . look like us.
(Bring the space person up out of the box.)
They have six arms!
(Point to each feature as it is mentioned.)

We have only two.
They have one eye, yellow and blue.
Two purple ears—both pointing south (point downward)
And a long, skinny tooth in a little round mouth.
Their nose looks like . . . a Brussels sprout!
And their hair keeps going in and out!
(Move dowel up and down.)

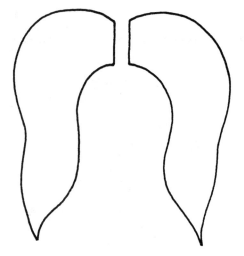

ears
(purple felt)

hand
cut 6
(felt)

tooth
(felt)

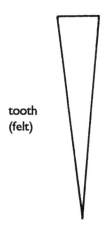

mouth
(felt)

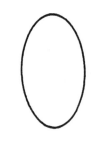

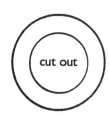

cut out

lip circle
(felt)

eyeball
(blue felt)

nose
cut 2
(green felt)

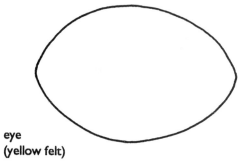

eye
(yellow felt)

148

THE STORM
MATERIALS

- patterns (pages 152 and 153)
- interfacing (10" x 12") (25.4 cm x 30.5 cm)
- posterboard (12" x 14") (30.5 cm x 35.5 cm)
- black permanent marker
- crayons
- gold glitter
- liquid glitter
- straw
- cotton balls
- self-adhesive Velcro (6-inch strip) (15.2 cm)
- silver, blue, or iridescent tinsel
- book tape
- paper plate (9") (22.9 cm)
- drawing compass
- paint or permanent markers
- paint stick
- black paint
- satin, gift-wrap, or iridescent ribbon (all the colors of the rainbow)

Sun Stick Puppet

1. Using a black marker, trace a sun (page 152) onto interfacing.
2. Color and glue the sun to posterboard.
3. Paint gold glitter on the sun, then cut the sun out.
4. Tape a straw to the back of the sun.

Cloud

1. Using a black marker, trace a cloud (page 153) onto interfacing.
2. Color and glue the cloud to posterboard.
3. Glue cotton balls to the front of the cloud.
4. Dab black paint on the cotton. Let the paint dry thoroughly and then cut the cloud out.
5. Cut a 2" x 4" (5.0 cm x 10.2 cm) strip of posterboard. Fold the strip in half, then turn up each end 1 inch (2.5 cm). Pinch the strip together in the center and tape the ends to the back of the cloud to make a handle.

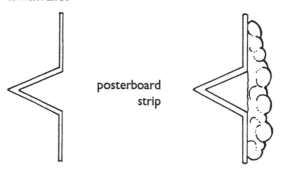

posterboard strip

6. Cut a 6-inch (15.2 cm) strip of Velcro in half lengthwise. Stick the hooked side to the back of the cloud where indicated.

Lightning

1. Using a black marker, trace the lightning (page 153) onto interfacing.
2. Color and glue the lightning to posterboard.
3. Paint gold glitter on the lightning, then cut the lightning out. (Do not color or glitter one tip of the lightning bolt so the Velcro will stick to it.)
4. Stick a $1/4$-inch (6 mm) square of the looped side of the Velcro to the tip of the lightning bolt where indicated by the dotted lines.

Far Out!

Rain

1. Cut a $1/2$" x 6" (1.3 cm x 15.2 cm) strip of posterboard. Glue 8-inch to 10-inch (20.3 cm to 25.4 cm) strands of silver, blue, or iridescent tinsel along the entire strip. Let the glue dry thoroughly.

2. Place the rain strip with the plain side of the posterboard facing up and the tinsel side facing down. Tape a 7-inch (17.7 cm) strip of book tape lengthwise along the posterboard strip so that half of it extends up above the top of the strip. Fold this length over the top edge of the strip and down over the glued tinsel strands on the other side. This will secure the tinsel in place. Cut off the excess tape at each end.
3. Stick a 6-inch (15.2 cm) strip of the looped side of the Velcro across the taped end of the rain strip.

Rainbow Stick Puppet

1. Place a paper plate bottom-side up on the table. Put the point of a drawing compass in the exact center of the plate. Starting $1/2$ inch (1.3 cm) in from the outer edge of the plate, draw seven circles, each $1/2$ inch (1.3 cm) smaller than the last.

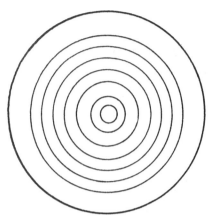

2. Using paint or permanent markers, color the circles, starting with red on the outside circle, then orange, yellow, green, blue, blue violet (indigo), with red-violet on the inside circle. The very center of the plate remains white.
3. Fold the plate in half with the painted side out. Cut a slit along the center of the fold, large enough to accommodate a paint stick. Insert the stick up into the rainbow. Tape the stick to one of the plate's unpainted interior surfaces and staple the plate together around the edge.
4. Glue ribbon along the flat edge of the paper-plate rainbow puppet. Match the ribbon color to the rainbow circle from which it descends. Cut several 2-foot (61 cm) ribbon strips and fold each strip in half. Glue the fold of the ribbon to the fold in the plate.
5. Paint the rainbow with liquid glitter.

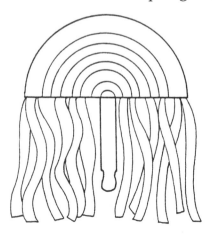

POEM

The Storm

One day the sun was shining bright.
(Hold up the sun.)
Then along came a cloud as black as
night.
(Hold up the cloud.)
Thunder crashed. Boom! Boom!
Boom!
Lightning flashed. Zoom! Zoom!
Zoom!
(Attach the lightning to the cloud.)

And then the rain came pouring
down.
(Attach the rain to the cloud.)
It rained and rained all over town.
At last the storm passed right
on by.
(Move the cloud behind your
back.)
And a beautiful rainbow filled the
sky.
(Hold up the rainbow.)

sun
(interfacing)

cloud
(interfacing)

place Velcro strip here

place Velcro here

lightning
(interfacing)

Far Out!

BOOK CORNER

Asch, Frank. *Happy Birthday, Moon.* Englewood Cliffs, NJ: Prentice-Hall, 1982.

Asch, Frank. *Mooncake.* Englewood Cliffs, NJ: Prentice-Hall, 1983.

Barrett, Judi. *Cloudy with a Chance of Meatballs.* New York, NY: Atheneum, 1978.

Barton, Byron. *I Want to Be an Astronaut.* New York, NY: Crowell, 1988.

Brown, Margaret Wise. *Wait Till the Moon Is Full.* New York, NY: Harper & Row, 1948.

Carle, Eric. *Papa, Please Get the Moon for Me.* Natick, ME: Picture Book Studio, 1986.

Chapman, Carol. *Barney Bipple's Magic Dandelions.* New York, NY: Dial, 1988.

Crowe, Robert L. *Tyler Toad and the Thunder.* New York, NY: E.P. Dutton, 1980.

Dayrell, Elphinstone. *Why the Sun and the Moon Live in the Sky.* Boston, MA: Houghton Mifflin, 1986.

Dragonwagon, Crescent. *Half a Moon and One Whole Star.* New York, NY: Macmillan, 1986.

Freeman, Don. *A Rainbow of My Own.* New York, NY: Viking, 1966.

Ginsburg, Mirra. *Where Does the Sun Go at Night?* New York, NY: Greenwillow Books, 1981.

Johnson, Crockett. *Harold's Trip to the Sky.* New York, NY: Harper & Row, 1957.

McDermott, Gerald. *Sun Flight.* New York, NY: Four Winds, 1980.

McPhail, David. *First Flight.* Boston, MA: Little, Brown, 1987.

Pinkwater, Daniel. *Guys from Space.* New York, NY: Macmillan, 1989.

Yolen, Jane. *Commander Toad in Space.* New York, NY: Coward-McCann, 1980.

Zolotow, Charlotte. *The Storm Book.* New York, NY: Harper & Row, 1952.

FLY AWAY

1. Make the box according to the instructions provided on page 16.
2. Cover the outside of the box with light blue felt.

A FAMILY OF OWLS

MATERIALS

- patterns (page 158)
- garden glove
- felt
  beige (4" x 7") (10.2 cm x 17.7 cm)
  gold scrap
  brown (3" x 6") (7.6 cm x 15.2 cm)
  green scrap
- pom-poms
  5 brown (1 1/2") (3.9 cm)
  5 brown (2") (5.0 cm)
- 10 owl or wiggly eyes (15 mm)

Owl Glove Puppet

1. Glue a 2-inch (5.0 cm) brown pom-pom to the fingernail side of each glove fingertip.
2. Glue a 1 1/2-inch (3.9 cm) brown pom-pom below each of the larger pom-poms for the owl bodies.
3. Glue each pair of pom-poms together, with the heads larger than the bodies.
4. Cut five owl faces (page 158) from beige felt, five beaks (page 158) from gold felt, and ten wings (page 158) from brown felt.
5. Glue the faces to the center of each 2-inch (5.0 cm) pom-pom.
6. Glue each beak to the lower center of the face where indicated by the dotted line.
7. Glue one wing to each side of the smaller pom-poms. Or use brown feathers, if you wish.
8. Glue two owl or wiggly eyes to each face.

9. Cut several leaves (page 158) from green felt and glue them to the glove fingertips at random.

A Family of Owls

A family of owls
(Hold up your gloved hand with
your fingers hidden.)
Lived high in a tree.
Father,
(Raise the thumb.)
Mother,
(Raise the index finger.)
And babies three.
(Raise the remaining fingers.)

Now, owls, as you know,
Sleep during the day.
(Lower the fingers.)
But when night comes
They like to play.
(Raise all the fingers again.)
Over the meadow they swoop and
glide.
(Fly your hand around.)

A Family of Owls continued

While mice and bunnies all run
and hide.
"Whoo, whoo!" calls the mother.
(Wiggle the index finger.)
"It's time to rest."
And the five little owls
(Flutter all the fingers as you
lower them into a fist again.)
Fly back to their nest.

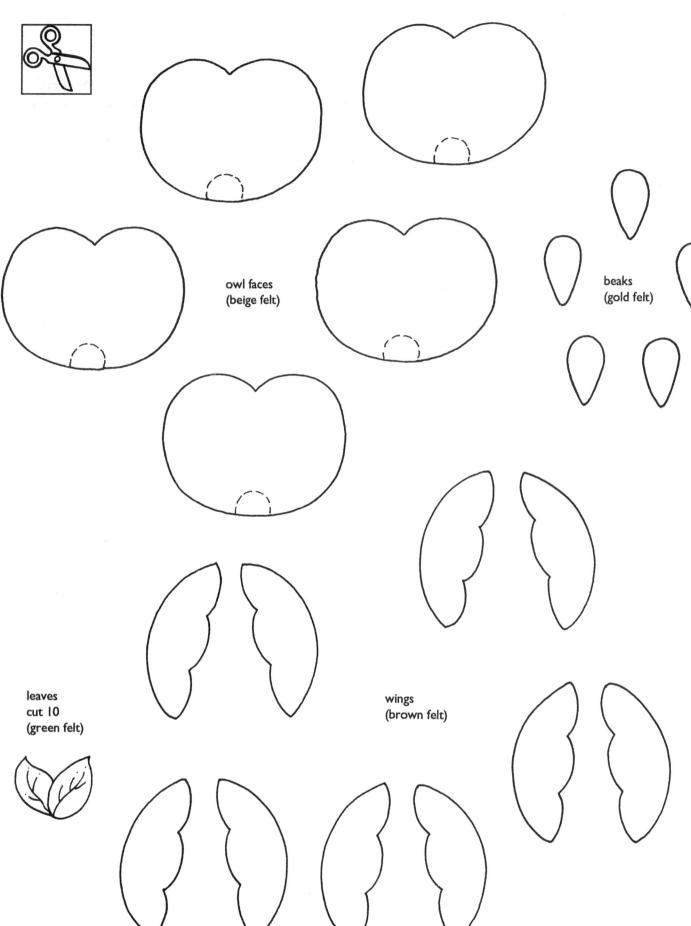

owl faces
(beige felt)

beaks
(gold felt)

leaves
cut 10
(green felt)

wings
(brown felt)

158

TWO LITTLE BLACKBIRDS

MATERIALS

- patterns (pages 161 and 162)
- paper cup (9 oz) (282 mL)
- felt
  green (8" x 10") (20.3 cm x 25.4 cm)
  brown (5" x 6") (12.7 cm x 15.2 cm)
  yellow scrap
- pom-poms
  2 black (1") (2.5 cm)
  2 black (1 1/2") (3.9 cm)
- 4 wiggly eyes (3 mm)
- posterboard (5" x 6") (12.7 cm x 15.2 cm)
- 2 bamboo skewers

Hill Cup

1. Cut out the cup cover (page 161) and cover the paper cup with green felt according to the instructions provided on page 25.
2. Cut one hill (page 162) from posterboard and one from brown felt. Glue the two hills together.
3. Glue the hill to the covered cup with the bottom edges of the hill even and the hilltop extending up above the top edge of the cup.

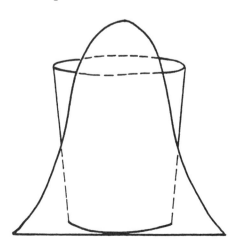

Blackbird Stick Puppets

1. Insert the pointed end of a bamboo skewer into the center of a 1 1/2-inch (3.9 cm) black pom-pom and glue the skewer in place. Repeat with a second skewer and pom-pom.
2. Glue a 1-inch (2.5 cm) black pom-pom to the top of each larger pom-pom.
3. Cut two beaks (page 162) from yellow felt. Fold each beak in half and glue in place on the small black pom-pom.
4. Glue two wiggly eyes to each small pom-pom.

5. Poke two holes, side by side, in the bottom of the cup.
6. Stick the skewers down inside the cup through the holes so the birds can hide down inside the cup until you push them up. Cut off the ends of the skewers so that only 3 inches (7.6 cm) protrude below the bottom of the cup when the birds are sitting on the hill.
7. Hold the cup with your index and second fingers along the bottom and your thumb at the back of the cup. The other two fingers should be together below the bottom of the cup, pushing lightly against the skewers to hold them in

place. Move the skewers up and down with your other hand to manipulate the birds.

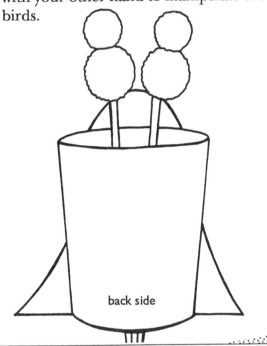

back side

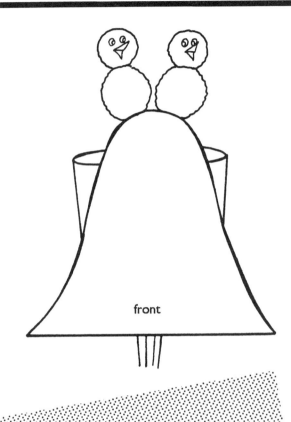

front

POEM

Two Little Blackbirds

Two little blackbirds
(Hold up the cup with the birds
perched on the hill.)
Sitting on a hill.
One named Jack,
(Wiggle the left bird.)
One named Jill.
(Wiggle the right bird.)

Fly away, Jack.
(Raise the left bird, then lower
into the cup.)
Fly away, Jill.
(Raise the right bird, then lower
into the cup.)
Come back, Jack. Come back, Jill.
(Perch the left bird back on the
hill and then perch the right bird
back on the hill.)

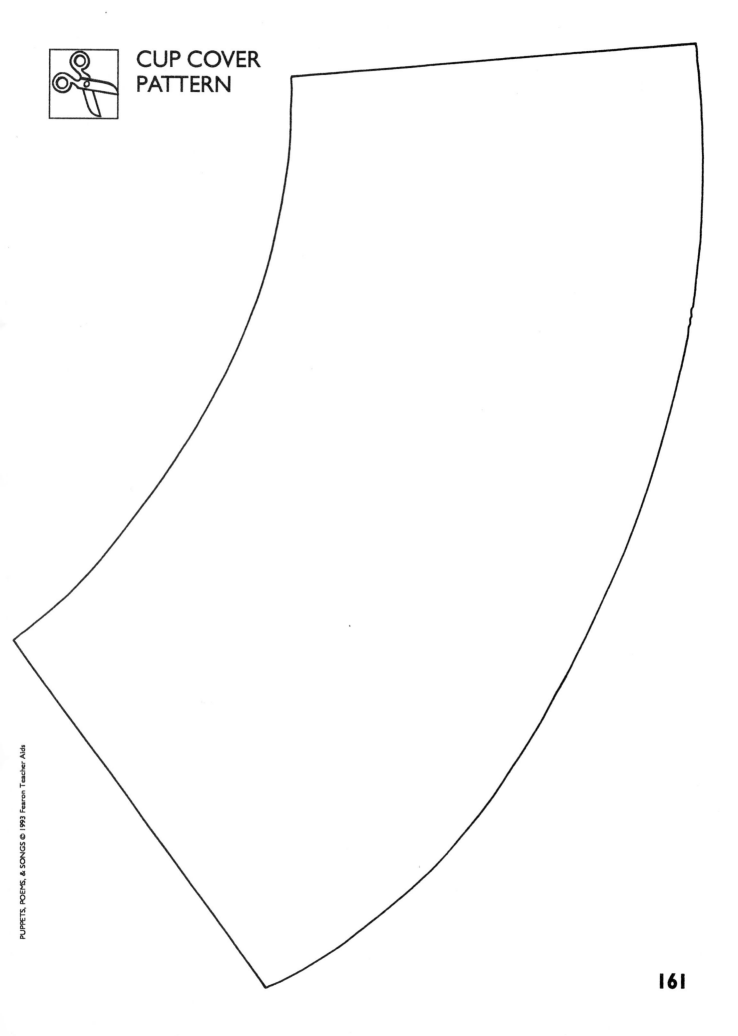

CUP COVER
PATTERN

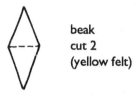

beak
cut 2
(yellow felt)

hill
cut 2
(posterboard/brown felt)

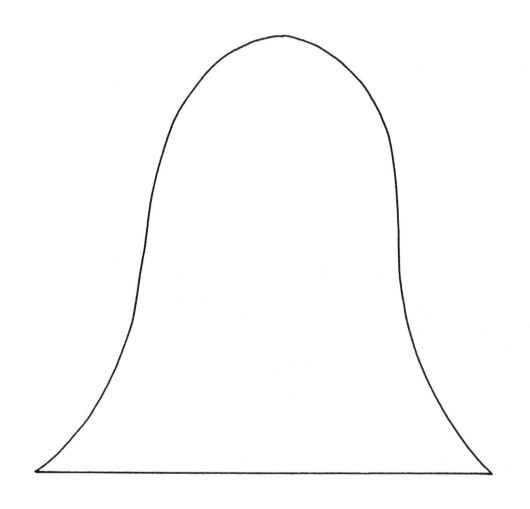

FIVE LITTLE BIRDS

MATERIALS

- pattern (page 164)
- garden glove
- yellow felt scrap
- pom-poms
  2 blue (1" and 1 1/2") (2.5 cm and 3.9 cm)
  2 red (1" and 1 1/2") (2.5 cm and 3.9 cm)
  2 light green (1" and 1 1/2") (2.5 cm and 3.9 cm)
  2 orange (1" and 1 1/2") (2.5 cm and 3.9 cm)
  2 pink (1" and 1 1/2") (2.5 cm and 3.9 cm)
- 10 wiggly eyes (3 mm)
- feathers

Bird Glove Puppet

1. Glue a 1-inch (2.5 cm) blue pom-pom to the glove index finger, a 1-inch (2.5 cm) red pom-pom to the second finger, a 1-inch (2.5 cm) light green pom-pom to the ring finger, a 1-inch (2.5 cm) orange pom-pom to the little finger, and a 1-inch (2.5 cm) pink pom-pom to the thumb.
2. Glue the 1 1/2-inch (3.9 cm) pom-poms below each smaller pom-pom of the same color. Glue each pair of pom-poms together.
3. Cut five beaks (page 164) from yellow felt.
4. Fold each beak in half and glue the beaks in place on the smaller pom-poms.
5. Glue two wiggly eyes to each bird above the beak.
6. Glue small, appropriately colored feathers to the sides of each body pom-pom for wings.

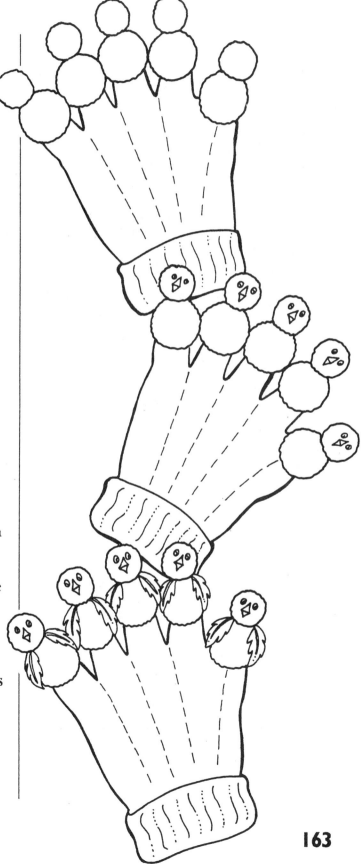

Fly Away

POEM

Five Little Birds

One little bird with lovely feathers blue.
(Hold up the index finger.)
He sat beside a red bird.
That made two.
(Hold up each finger in turn.)
Two little birds singing in a tree.
A green one came to join them.
That made three.
Three little birds, wishing there were more.

Along came an orange bird.
That made four.
Four little birds, glad to be alive.
Along came a pink bird.
That made five.
Five little birds sang happy songs all day.
Then five little birds spread their wings
And flew away.
(Fly the glove behind your back.)

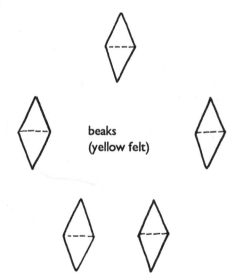

beaks
(yellow felt)

IF I WERE A BUTTERFLY

MATERIALS

- patterns (page 167)
- several bright colors of felt
- 2 wiggly eyes (7 mm)
- pom-pom ($^1/_4$") (6 mm)
- decorating trim, such as sequins, glitter, felt shapes, rickrack, and fabric paint

Butterfly Finger Puppet

1. Cut two butterfly bodies (page 167) from brightly colored felt.
2. Cut four wings (page 167) from a different color felt than the body. Glue each pair of wings together.
3. Cut two antennae (page 167) from another felt color.
4. Glue the left and right wings in position on one body piece where indicated by the dotted lines.
5. Glue the antennae in position on the body where indicated by the dotted lines (see illustration upper right).
6. Draw a thin line of glue around the outside edge of the body piece that has wings and antennae attached. Place the second body piece on top, sandwiching the pieces between the butterfly bodies. Do not glue the bottom of the butterfly body together. Leave the end open so you can stick your finger inside the puppet body.

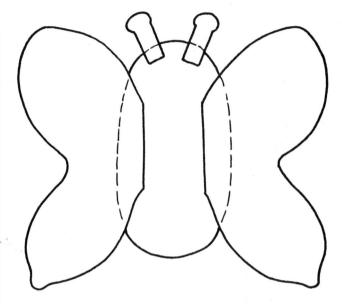

7. Glue two wiggly eyes and a $^1/_4$-inch (6 mm) pom-pom to the butterfly's face. Allow the glue to dry thoroughly.
8. Decorate the wings with a trim of your choice.

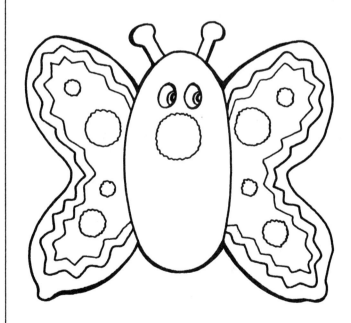

PUPPETS, POEMS, & SONGS © 1993 Fearon Teacher Aids

POEM

If I Were a Butterfly

If I were a butterfly,
I'd flutter all around.
(Flutter the butterfly on your
index finger.)
I'd sip the nectar from the flowers
And never make a sound.
My wings would sparkle in the sun,
so fairy-like and bright.
I'd love to be a butterfly,
A creature of delight.

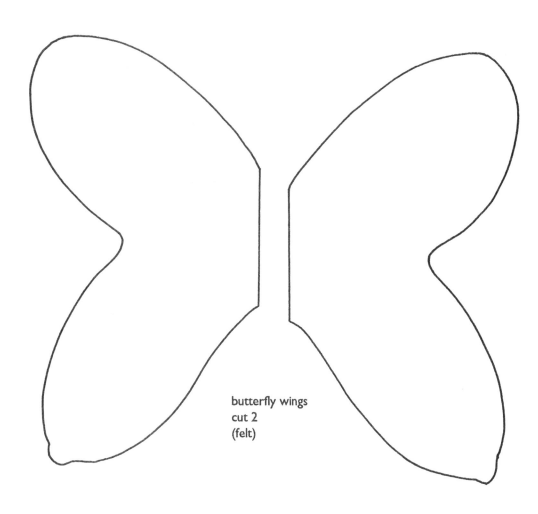

butterfly wings
cut 2
(felt)

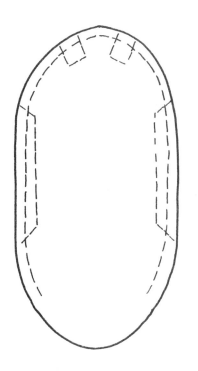

butterfly body
cut 2
(felt)

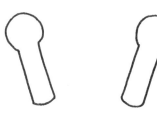

antennae
(felt)

Fly Away

FIVE BUSY BEES
MATERIALS

- patterns (page 170)
- garden glove
- felt
  tan or gold (4" x 4") (10.2 cm x 10.2 cm)
  black scrap
- pom-poms
  5 yellow (1") (2.5 cm)
  5 yellow (1 1/2") (3.9 cm)
- interfacing (3" x 7") (7.6 cm x 17.7 cm)
- black permanent marker
- black yarn
- 10 eyes (10 mm)

Bee Glove Puppet

1. Cut a beehive (page 170) from tan or gold felt.
2. Cut a small hole in the beehive and glue a small piece of black felt behind the hole.
3. Glue the beehive to the center back of the glove, with the bottom edge along the seam where the cuff joins the glove body.

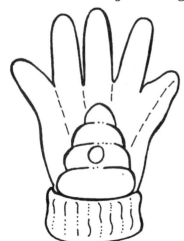

4. Glue a 1-inch (2.5 cm) yellow pom-pom to the fingernail side of each glove fingertip.

5. Using a black marker, trace five wings (page 170) onto interfacing. Then cut the wings out.
6. Glue a pair of interfacing wings to each fingertip with the center top edge just slightly up under the 1-inch (2.5 cm) head pom-pom.
7. Glue a 1 1/2-inch (3.9 cm) yellow pom-pom on top of the wings and beneath each of the smaller pom-poms.
8. Glue each pair of pom-poms together.
9. Cut lengths of fuzzy black yarn and glue three across and around each bee body for stripes.
10. Cut ten more short pieces of black yarn and glue two to the top of each bee head for antennae.

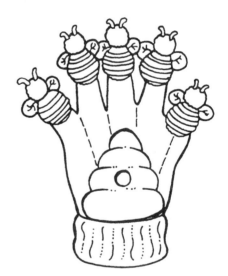

11. Glue two eyes to each bee head.

Five Busy Bees

Five busy bees on a lovely
spring day.
(Hold up the gloved fingers.)
This one said, "Let's fly away!"
(Indicate each bee in turn.)
This one said, "We'll drink some
nectar sweet."
This one said, "Let's get pollen on
our feet."
This one said, "And then we'll make
some honey."

This one said, "Good thing it's
warm and sunny."
So the five busy bees went flying
along
(Fly your hand around while
wiggling fingers.)
Singing a happy honeybee song.
Bzzzzzzzzzz!
(Fly your hand behind your back.)

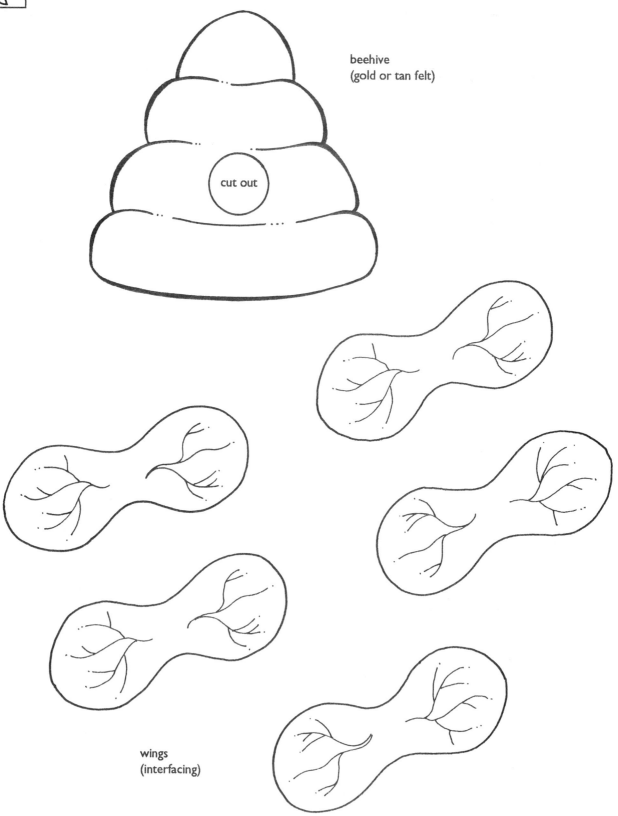

beehive
(gold or tan felt)

cut out

wings
(interfacing)

PUPPETS, POEMS, & SONGS © 1993 Fearon Teacher Aids

BUZZ BUZZ BUZZ

MATERIALS

- patterns (page 173)
- 2 paper plates (7") (17.7 cm)
- felt
  black scraps
  yellow (3" x 4") (7.6 cm x 10.2 cm)
  green (4" x 5") (10.2 cm x 12.7 cm)
- pom-poms
  1 yellow (1 1/2") (3.9 cm)
  1 orange (5 mm)
- wiggly eyes
  2 (8 mm)
  2 (20 mm)
- paint (red and green)
- interfacing (2" x 5") (5.0 cm x 12.7 cm)
- black permanent marker
- black yarn
- fake eyelashes
- wooden dowel (1/4" x 12") (6 mm x 30.5 cm)
- decorating materials, such as feathers, pom-poms, rickrack, and sequins

Bee Finger Puppet

1. Cut three bee stripes (page 173) from black felt.
2. Cut the bee body (page 173) from yellow felt.
3. Glue the stripes to the body and then glue the bee body together, overlapping the edges along the dotted line to make a tube shape.
4. Separate the fibers of a 1 1/2-inch (3.9 cm) yellow pom-pom until you reach the center. Fill the center with glue. Pinch the top of the bee body tube together. Place the top of the body tube into the glued center of the pom-pom. Close the

pom-pom fibers back over the tube. Set the figure aside to dry.

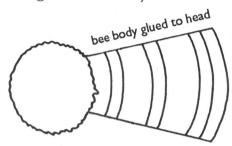

bee body glued to head

5. Place the straight edge of the bee wing on the fold of the interfacing as indicated. Using a black marker, trace the wings (page 173) onto interfacing. Then cut the wings out.
6. Glue the wings to the center back of the body tube. The bee body seam should be on the underside of the bee.
7. Glue the orange pom-pom to the center of the bee face.
8. Glue two wiggly eyes (8 mm) above the orange pom-pom on either side.
9. Cut two 1 1/2-inch (3.9 cm) pieces of black yarn. Separate the fibers of the yellow pom-pom on top of the bee's head, above the eyes. Dip the ends of the yarn into glue and insert the glued yarn into the holes on top of the head pompom for antennae.

Fly Away

Flower Paper-Plate Puppet

1. Paint the bottoms of two paper plates red. Let the paint dry thoroughly. (You may want to use party plates from card shops because they already have scalloped edges that look like petals and they're extra sturdy.)
2. Decorate the center of the red side of one plate with felt, wiggly eyes (20 mm), fake eyelashes, pom-poms, feathers, rickrack, and sequins to make the flower's face.
3. Paint a wooden dowel green. Let the paint dry thoroughly.
4. Cut two leaves (page 173) from green felt.
5. Tape one end of the dowel to the unpainted side of the paper plate without the face.

6. Place the face plate on top of the back plate, sandwiching the dowel in between. Staple or glue the plates together around the edges. If you use the scalloped plates, be sure to match the scallops.
7. Glue the two leaves to the dowel just below the plates.

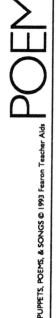

POEM

Buzz, Buzz, Buzz

"Buzz, buzz, buzz,"
Said a bright yellow bee.
(Hold up the bee on your index finger.)
And he was looking straight at me!
He flew and he flew all around my head
(Fly the bee around your head.)
And then he spied a flower so red.
(Hold up the flower.)
He tickled her face with his tiny feet

(Move the bee around on the flower's face.)
While he gathered nectar sweet.
And then, when that little bee was through,
He gave her a kiss
(Have the bee kiss the flower.)
And away he flew.
(Fly the bee behind your back.)

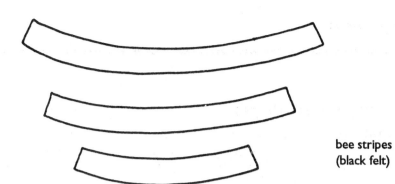

bee stripes
(black felt)

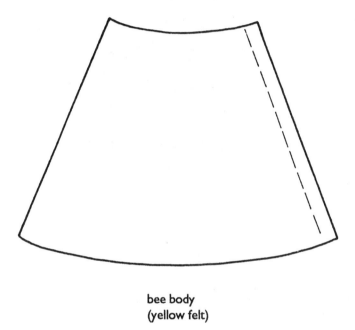

bee body
(yellow felt)

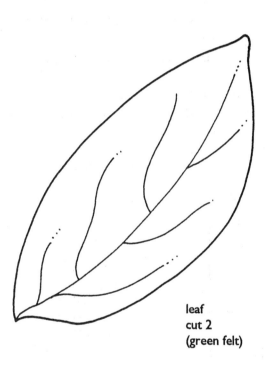

leaf
cut 2
(green felt)

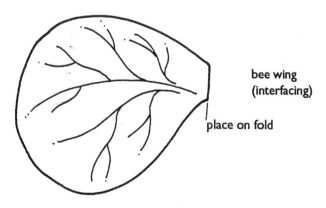

bee wing
(interfacing)

place on fold

Fly Away

HERE IS AN OWL

MATERIALS

- patterns (pages 176 and 177)
- 4 paper plates (9") (22.9 cm)
- paint (brown and gold)
- 2 wiggly eyes (40 mm)

Owl Paper-Plate Puppet

1. Paint the bottom of one paper plate brown and paint the bottom of two paper plates gold. Let the paint dry thoroughly.
2. Trace two claws (page 176), two wings (page 176), two eye sockets (page 177), two tufts (page 177), two eyelids (page 177), and one beak (page 177) onto the gold plates. Add depth and texture to the puppet parts by placing the patterns on the natural curves around the edges of the plates. Cut the pieces out.
3. Staple the tufts to the top of the unpainted side of the brown paper plate.
4. Staple the claws to the bottom of the same plate.
5. Glue the eye sockets close together in the center top of the plate.
6. Glue two wiggly eyes to the center of the socket circles and glue the eyelids over the top part of the socket and eyes.
7. Glue the beak to the center of the face between the eye sockets, pointing towards the claws.

8. Fit the unpainted paper plate to the back of the owl plate and staple around the edges, except at the bottom. Leave enough area unstapled to fit your hand up into the puppet between the plates.
9. Glue the wings to the sides of the puppet body, extending beyond the edge of the plates.
10. Paint or draw pointed lines on the body to indicate feathers. Or, glue real feathers on the body, if possible.

174

POEM

Here Is an Owl

Here is an owl
(Hold up the owl.)
He sits in a tree.
He blinks his eyes so sleepily.
He has a sharp beak instead of a nose.
(Point out each feature.)

And sharp, pointed claws instead of toes.
He looks at me and he looks at you.
He ruffles his feathers and says, "Whoo, whoo."

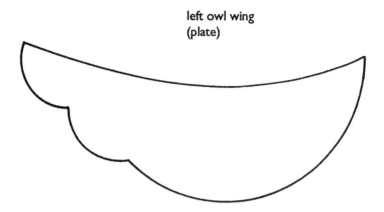

left owl wing
(plate)

right owl wing
(plate)

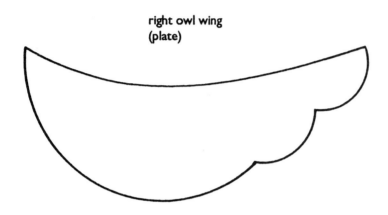

owl claw
cut 2
(plate)

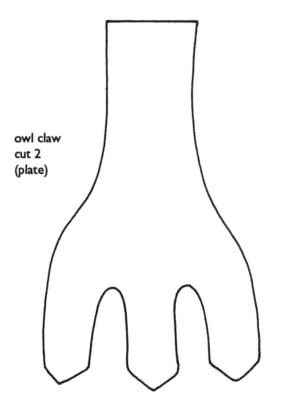

owl eye socket
cut 2
(plate)

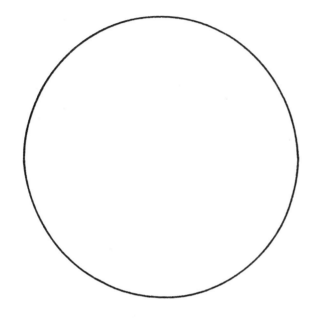

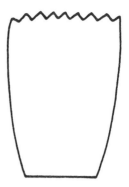

owl tuft
cut 2
(plate)

owl beak
(plate)

owl eyelid
cut 2
(plate)

SING A SONG OF SIXPENCE

MATERIALS

- patterns (pages 180 and 181)
- interfacing (10" x 11") (25.4 cm x 28 cm)
- posterboard (10" x 11") (25.4 cm x 28 cm)
- black permanent marker
- crayons
- brad fastener
- self-adhesive Velcro ($^1/_2$-inch square) (1.3 cm)

Pie

1. Using a black marker, trace the pie plate (page 180) and pie crust (page 181) onto interfacing.
2. Color and glue the figures to posterboard, then cut the figures out.
3. Poke a hole through the dot on each piece.
4. Fit the pie crust over the pie plate, matching the dots, and insert a brad fastener through the holes to make a hinge.
5. Stick the hooked side of a Velcro square to the front rim of the pie plate where indicated. (The Velcro will stick to the interfacing much better if you don't color the interfacing in that spot.)
6. Stick the looped side of a Velcro square to the matching backside of the pie crust where indicated.
7. Connect the Velcro squares on the pie plate and the pie crust so the pie will stay in place properly until you are ready to swing the crust up and reveal the blackbirds in the pie.

PUPPETS, POEMS, & SONGS © 1993 Fearon Teacher Aids

POEM

Sing a Song of Sixpence

Sing a song of sixpence,
A pocket full of rye;
Four-and-twenty blackbirds
(Hold up the pie.)
Baked in a pie.
When the pie was opened
(Open the pie.)
The birds began to sing;
Wasn't that a dainty dish
To set before the king?

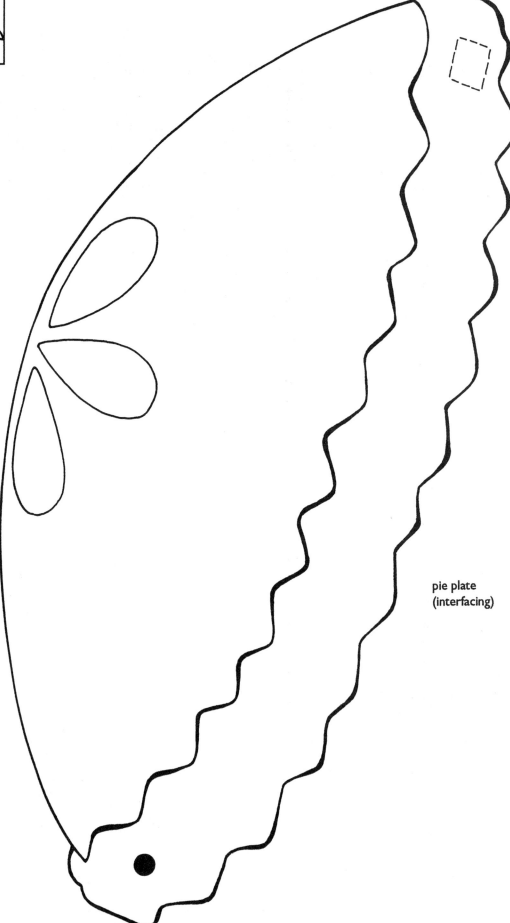

place Velcro here

pie plate
(interfacing)

PUPPETS, POEMS, & SONGS © 1993 Fearon Teacher Aids

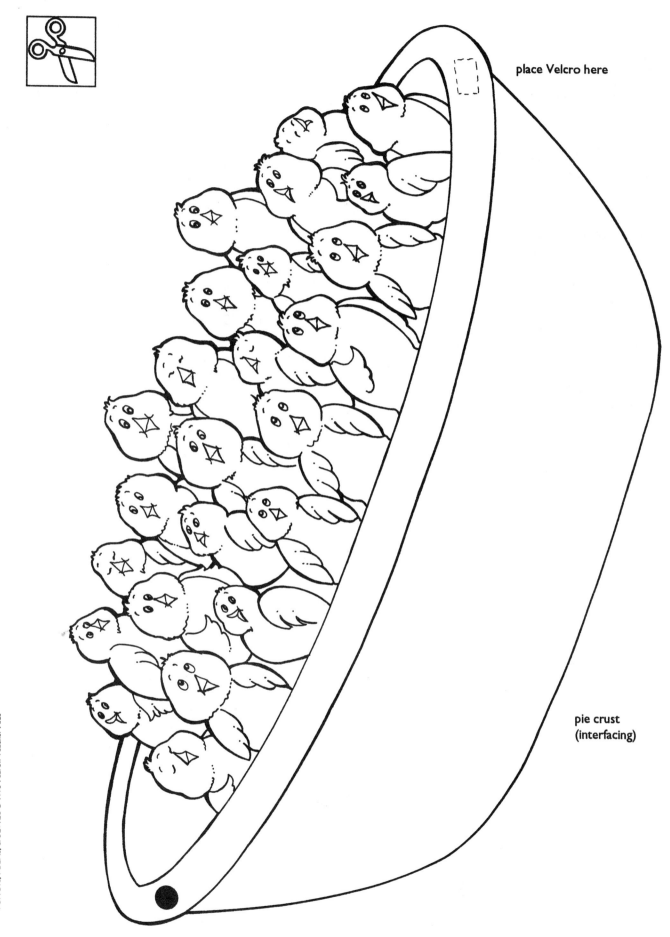

place Velcro here

pie crust
(interfacing)

BOOK CORNER

Arnold, Caroline. *Five Nests*. New York, NY: E.P. Dutton, 1980.

Banks, Merry. *Animals of the Night*. New York, NY: Charles Scribner's Sons, 1990.

Brown, Ruth. *Ladybug, Ladybug*. New York, NY: E.P. Dutton, 1988.

Carle, Eric. *The Grouchy Ladybug*. New York, NY: Crowell, 1977.

Denslow, Sharon Phillips. *Night Owls*. New York, NY: Bradbury Press, 1990.

Eastman, P.D. *The Best Nest*. New York, NY: Random House, 1968.

Eastman, P.D. *Are You My Mother?* New York, NY: Random House, 1960.

Emberley, Ed. *The Wing on a Flea*. Boston, MA: Little, Brown, 1961.

Flack, Marjorie. *The Story About Ping*. New York, NY: Viking, 1933.

Freeman, Don. *Fly High, Fly Low*. New York, NY: Viking, 1957.

Howe, James. *I Wish I Were a Butterfly*. New York, NY: Harcourt Brace Jovanovich, 1987.

Hutchins, Pat. *Good-Night, Owl!* New York, NY: Macmillan, 1972.

Kraus, Robert. *Owliver*. New York, NY: Windmill, 1974.

Lobel, Arnold. *Owl at Home*. New York, NY: Harper & Row, 1975.

McClintock, Marshall. *A Fly Went By*. New York, NY: Random House, 1958.

Peet, Bill. *Fly, Homer, Fly*. Boston, MA: Houghton Mifflin, 1969.

Preston, Edna. *The Sad Story of the Little Bluebird and the Hungry Cat*. New York, NY: Four Winds, 1975.

FURRY FRIENDS

1. Make the box according to the instructions provided on page 16.
2. Cover the outside of the box with brown felt.

FIVE LITTLE MICE

MATERIALS

- patterns (page 186)
- garden glove
- felt
  gray (5" x 7") (12.7 cm x 17.7 cm)
  pink scrap
- pom-poms
  5 gray (1 1/2") (3.9 cm)
  5 gray (3/4") (1.9 cm)
- 5 half-rounds (6 mm)
- 10 wiggly eyes (6 mm)
- black carpet thread
- calico ribbon (#9)
- kitchen miniatures—a broom, cake, and cheese

Mice Glove Puppet

1. Glue a 1 1/2-inch (3.9 cm) gray pom-pom to the fingernail side of each glove fingertip.
2. Glue a 3/4-inch (1.9 cm) pom-pom to the center of each larger pom-pom.
3. Cut three 1-inch (2.5 cm) strands of black carpet thread for each mouse.
4. Place a dot of glue on the front of each small pom-pom, just above the center.
5. Place three strands of thread on each small pom-pom, with the centers of the threads in the glue.
6. Glue a half-round over the threads' center for a nose.
7. Glue two wiggly eyes to each large pom-pom, close to the nose pom-pom.
8. Cut ten outer ears (page 186) from gray felt and ten inner ears (page 186) from pink felt.

9. Glue the inner ears to the outer ears. Glue the assembled ears to the sides of each head pom-pom.

10. Make a dress and arms (see patterns on page 186) from calico ribbon and hands from gray felt for each mouse.
11. Glue a miniature broom to the sweeping mouse, a miniature cake to the second mouse, and a miniature cheese or platter of cheeses to the fourth mouse.

PUPPETS, POEMS, & SONGS © 1993 Fearon Teacher Aids

POEM

Five Little Mice

Five little mice scampered
through the door.
(Hold up your gloved hand.)
This little mouse said, "It's time
to sweep the floor."
(Point to each mouse in turn.)
This little mouse said, "Look, I
baked a cake."
This little mouse not a sound did
make.

This little mouse said, "Why don't
we have some cheese?"
This little mouse heard a kitten
sneeze.
"Ah-choo!" sneezed the kitten.
"Eeeeeek!" the mice cried.
(Raise your hand and wiggle the
fingers.)
And they all scampered back to
their hole to hide.
(Run your hand behind your back.)

outer ear
cut 10
(gray felt)

inner ear
cut 10
(pink felt)

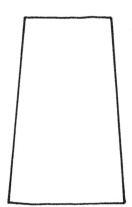

dress
cut 5
(adjust length as desired)

hand
cut 10
(gray felt)

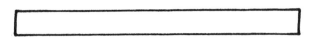

arm
cut 10

PUPPETS, POEMS, & SONGS © 1993 Fearon Teacher Aids

FIVE LITTLE MONKEYS

MATERIALS

- patterns (page 189)
- garden glove
- felt
  tan (3" x 6") (7.6 cm x 15.2 cm)
  brown (2" x 5") (5.0 cm x 12.7 cm)
- 5 brown pom-poms (1 1/2") (3.9 cm)
- 10 half-rounds (3 mm)
- 10 small black beads
- pink embroidery floss

MONKEY GLOVE PUPPET

1. Glue a 1 1/2-inch (3.9 cm) brown pom-pom to the fingernail side of each glove fingertip.
2. Cut five monkey faces (page 189) from tan felt.
3. Glue a face to each 1 1/2-inch (3.9 cm) brown pom-pom on the garden glove.
4. Glue two half-rounds on each face for eyes.
5. Glue two black beads on each face for nostrils.
6. Cut ten outer ears (page 189) from brown felt and ten inner ears (page 189) from tan felt.
7. Glue the inner ears to the outer ears and glue the assembled ears to the top front of each side of the monkeys' heads.

8. Draw a smiling mouth with glue and place a curving piece of pink embroidery floss in the glue. Use a piece of floss longer than you need for the mouth. Cut off the excess floss when the glue is dry.

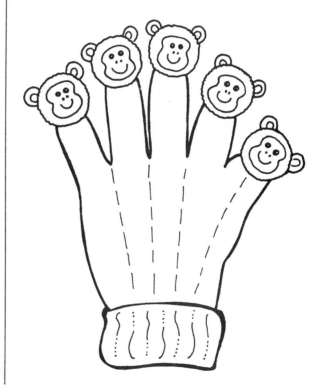

Furry Friends

PUPPETS, POEMS, & SONGS © 1993 Fearon Teacher Aids

Five Little Monkeys

Five little monkeys jumping on the bed.
(Hold up your gloved hand and jump the monkeys up and down.)
One fell off
(Hide the thumb.)
And he bumped his head.
(Tap the head with your other fist.)
Momma called the doctor

(Inscribe a circle in the air with your free index finger, as if dialing a phone.)
And the doctor said,
"No more monkeys jumping on the bed!"
(Shake your free index finger in a warning gesture.)
Four little monkeys jumping on the bed . . .

Five Little Monkeys continued

(Continue for each verse following previous instructions.)

Three little monkeys jumping on the bed . . .

Two little monkeys jumping on the bed . . .

One little monkey jumping on the bed . . .

PUPPETS, POEMS, & SONGS © 1993 Fearon Teacher Aids

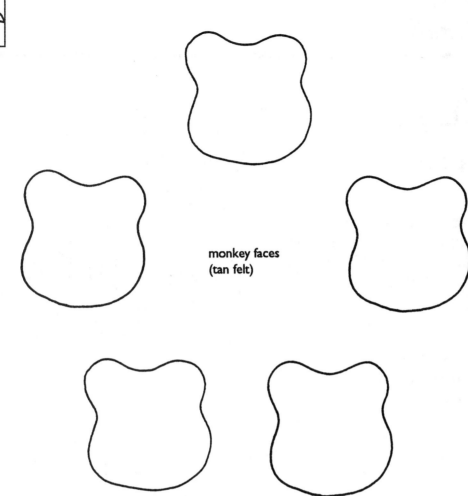

monkey faces
(tan felt)

outer ear
cut 10
(brown felt)

inner ear
cut 10
(tan felt)

Furry Friends

FIVE LITTLE PUPPIES

MATERIALS

- patterns (page 191)
- garden glove
- felt
  brown (3" x 5") (7.6 cm x 12.7 cm)
  beige or pink (3" x 5") (7.6 cm x 12.7 cm)
- 5 beige or pink pom-poms ($^1/_4$") (6 mm)
- 10 wiggly eyes (7 mm)
- red satin ribbon ($^1/_4$-inch wide) (6 mm)

Puppy Glove Puppet

1. Cut ten outer ears (page 191) from brown felt and ten inner ears (page 191) from beige or pink felt.
2. Glue an inner ear to each outer ear.
3. Glue two wiggly eyes to each glove finger.
4. Glue a $^1/_4$-inch (6 mm) beige or pink pom-pom (or a 10 mm animal nose with the stem cut off flush with the back of the nose) to each finger below the eyes.
5. Glue a strip of red satin ribbon around each finger, below the dog's face, like a collar around the dog's neck.
6. Glue the ears to the sides of the glove fingers, slightly above the eyes.

PUPPETS, POEMS, & SONGS © 1993 Fearon Teacher Aids

POEM

Five Little Puppies

Five little puppies barking at the door.
(Hold up your gloved hand.)
One chased his tail, and then there were four.
(Lower one finger at a time.)
Four little puppies barking up a tree,
One chased a cat and then there were three.

Three little puppies chewing on a shoe.
One chased a butterfly and then there were two.
Two little puppies gnawing on a bone.
One chased a squirrel and then there was one.
One little puppy snoozing in the sun.
She ran home for supper and then there were none.

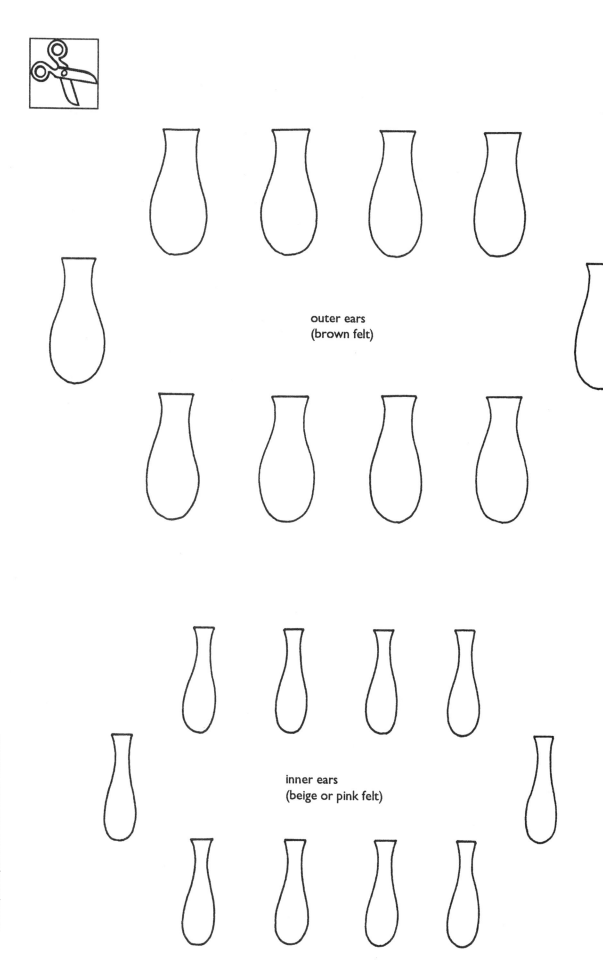

outer ears
(brown felt)

inner ears
(beige or pink felt)

ONCE UPON A TIME
MATERIALS

- patterns (page 194)
- garden glove
- felt
  black (3" x 4") (7.6 cm x 10.2 cm)
  pink (3" x 4") (7.6 cm x 10.2 cm)
- pom-poms
  1 black (2") (5.0 cm)
  3 black (1 1/2") (3.9 cm)
  9 white (1/4") (6 mm)
  3 white (1/2") (1.3 cm)
- 8 cat eyes (9 mm)
- fine monofilament fishing line
- yarn

Cat and Kitten Glove Puppet

1. Glue a 2-inch (5.0 cm) black pom-pom to the index fingertip for the cat and glue a 1 1/2-inch (3.9 cm) black pom-pom to the second, ring, and little fingertips for the kittens. Glue nothing to the thumb.
2. Glue three 1/4-inch (6 mm) white pom-poms in a triangle in the lower center of each 1 1/2-inch (3.9 cm) black pom-pom. Glue three 1/2-inch (1.3 cm) white pom-poms to the 2-inch (5.0 cm) black pom-pom. Glue the small pom-poms to each other as well as to the larger pom-pom.
3. Cut eight outer ears (page 194) from black felt. Cut four noses (page 194) and eight inner ears (page 194) from pink felt.
4. Glue each nose to the center top of the white pom-poms, with the point of the nose coming forward and down over the space between the two side-by-side pom-poms.
5. Glue the inner ears to the outer ears. Glue the assembled ears to the top of each cat's head.
6. Glue two cat eyes to each head pom-pom just above the nose pom-poms.
7. Glue lengths of fishing line to the two nose pom-poms for the whiskers.

Sweaters

1. If you know how to knit, knit three 1" x 2" (2.5 cm x 5.0 cm) rectangles out of any bright color yarn. If you don't know how to knit, cut three rectangles from something knitted out of wool or acrylic yarn, such as a scarf, gloves, or hat.
2. Glue the knitted rectangles lengthwise beneath the three smaller cat heads.
3. Roll more of the same color yarn into a 1 1/2-inch (3.9 cm) ball, leaving a 6-inch (15.2 cm) string coming off the end.
4. Glue the yarn ball to the center back of the glove and glue the loose end to the large cat's mouth.

POEM

PUPPETS, POEMS, & SONGS © 1993 Fearon Teacher Aids

Once Upon a Time

Once upon a time, there was a cat
(Hold up your gloved index finger.)
Who swallowed a whole ball of yarn!
And when that cat had baby kittens,
They all came with sweaters on!
(Raise the remaining kittens.)

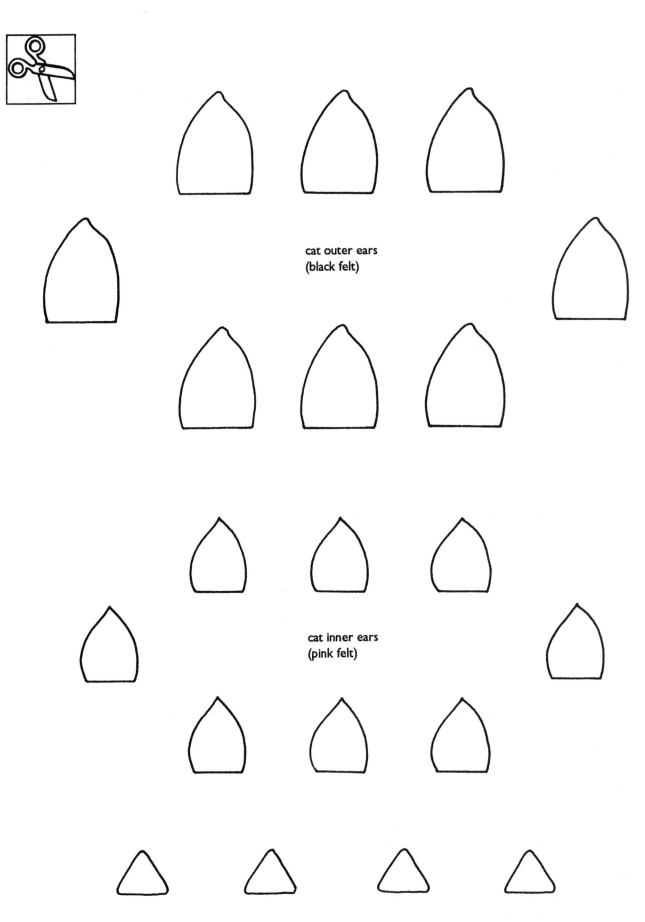

cat outer ears
(black felt)

cat inner ears
(pink felt)

cat noses
(pink felt)

PUPPETS, POEMS, & SONGS © 1993 Fearon Teacher Aids

TEASING MR. CROCODILE

MATERIALS

- patterns (pages 198 and 199)
- garden glove
- green sock
- felt
  green (8" x 10") (20.3 cm x 25.4 cm)
  tan (3" x 6") (7.6 cm x 15.2 cm)
  brown (2" x 5") (5.0 cm x 12.7 cm)
  pink (two 8" x 8" squares) (20.3 cm x 20.3 cm)
  white scrap
  black scrap
- 5 brown pom-poms (1 1/2") (3.9 cm)
- 10 half-rounds (3 mm)
- 2 eyes (30 mm)
- 10 small black beads
- pink embroidery floss
- 5 squares of black Velcro (1/2") (1.3 cm)
- posterboard (8" x 10") (20.3 cm x 25.4 cm)
- interfacing (8" x 8") (20.3 cm x 20.3 cm)
- pencil or dark chalk
- fiberfill
- hot glue gun

Tree

1. Cut one tree (page 199) from posterboard and one tree pattern from green felt.
2. Cut out the holes in the posterboard tree.
3. Glue the green felt to the posterboard and cut out the same holes. If using a right-handed glove, glue the green felt to the side of the posterboard in which the thumb hole is on your right. If using a left-handed glove, glue the green felt to the side of the posterboard in which the thumb hole is on your left.

Monkey Glove Puppet

1. Cut five monkey faces (page 198) from tan felt.
2. Glue each face to a 1 1/2-inch (3.9 cm) brown pom-pom.
3. Glue two half-rounds to each monkey face for eyes.
4. Glue two black beads on each monkey face for nostrils.
5. Cut ten outer ears (page 198) from brown felt and ten inner ears (page 198) from tan felt.
6. Glue the inner ears to the outer ears and glue the assembled ears to the top front of each side of the monkeys' heads.
7. Draw a smiling mouth with glue and place a curving piece of pink embroidery floss in the glue. Use a piece of floss longer than you need for the mouth. Then cut off the excess floss when the glue is dry.

8. Stick the hooked side of a Velcro square to the back of each monkey's head.
9. Stick the matching looped side of the Velcro square to the palm side of each glove fingertip. (This is an exception to the general rule for making glove puppets.)

Furry Friends

Mr. Crocodile Sock Puppet

1. Place a green sock on the table in front of you.
2. Beginning at the toe end, cut in towards the heel as indicated in the illustration on the right by the dotted line. Do not cut farther than the middle of the instep of the sock.
3. Spread the sock out flat so that the heel bulge is on the top.
4. Place a square of interfacing between two pink squares of felt. Fold the assembled square in half. Put the folded edge inside the sock opening so that the folded edge fits all the way back against the end of the cut in the sock.
5. Draw around the sock edge onto the felt with a pencil or dark chalk.
6. Remove the square and cut the folded shape out.
7. Glue one of the pink, felt mouth pieces to the interfacing. Place this glued mouth piece (interfacing side up) into the opened sock mouth. Pull the sock edges around the interfacing mouth edges and glue into place with a hot glue gun.
8. Glue the second pink felt mouth shape into the same opening on top of the mouth you just glued into place to cover up the raw edges of the sock.
9. Stuff a small amount of fiberfill into the heel and upper part of the toe to give the head shape.
10. Glue an eye to each side of the head.
11. Cut two teeth strips (page 198) from white felt. (Each strip should be long enough to fit all the way around the mouth.)

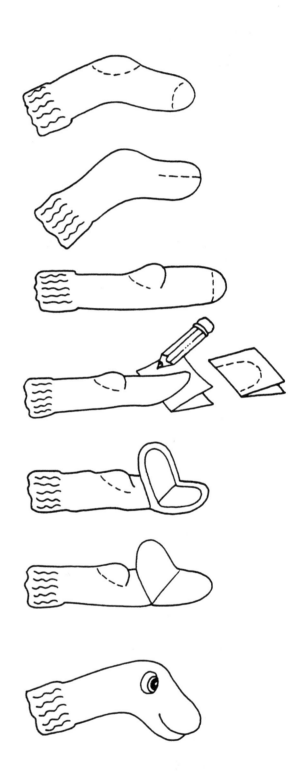

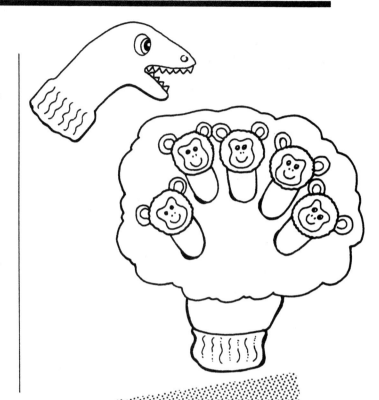

12. Glue one tooth strip around the top jaw (with teeth pointing down). Glue the other tooth strip around the bottom jaw (with teeth pointing up).

13. Cut two circles from black felt and glue one to each side of the front of the top jaw for nostrils.

14. Insert your hand into the puppet. The thumb works the bottom jaw and the fingers work the upper jaw.

15. Slip your gloved fingers through the holes in the tree and attach the monkey heads to the glove. Put the crocodile puppet on the other hand.

POEM

PUPPETS, POEMS, & SONGS © 1993 Fearon Teacher Aids

Teasing Mr. Crocodile

Five little monkeys sitting in a tree.
(Hold up the monkey glove puppet inserted into the tree finger holes.)
Teasing Mr. Crocodile, "You can't catch me.
You can't catch me, no,
(Raise the crocodile puppet and, on the word "SNAP," remove one monkey head with the crocodile mouth and have the crocodile sink back down into the box. Drop the monkey head in the box and repeat this action four more times.)

Four little monkeys sitting in a tree . . .

Three little monkeys sitting in a tree . . .

Two little monkeys sitting in a tree . . .

One little monkey sitting in a tree . . .

No little monkeys sitting in a tree.
I'd better run away so he won't catch me!

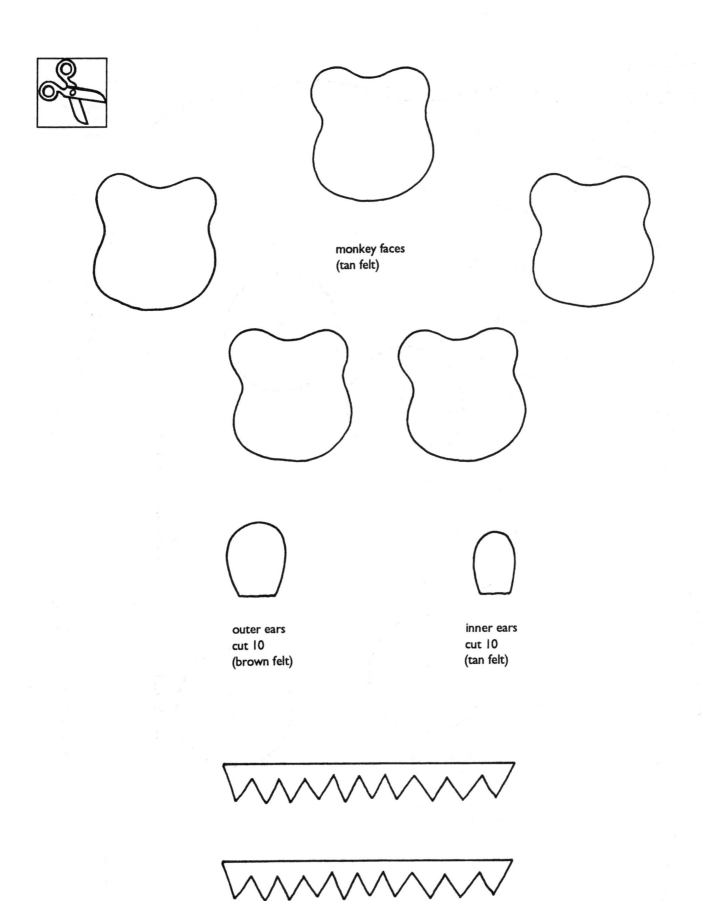

monkey faces
(tan felt)

outer ears
cut 10
(brown felt)

inner ears
cut 10
(tan felt)

teeth strips
(white felt)

PUPPETS, POEMS, & SONGS © 1993 Fearon Teacher Aids

cut out

cut out

cut out

cut out

cut out

tree
cut 2
(posterboard/green felt)

(thumb hole)

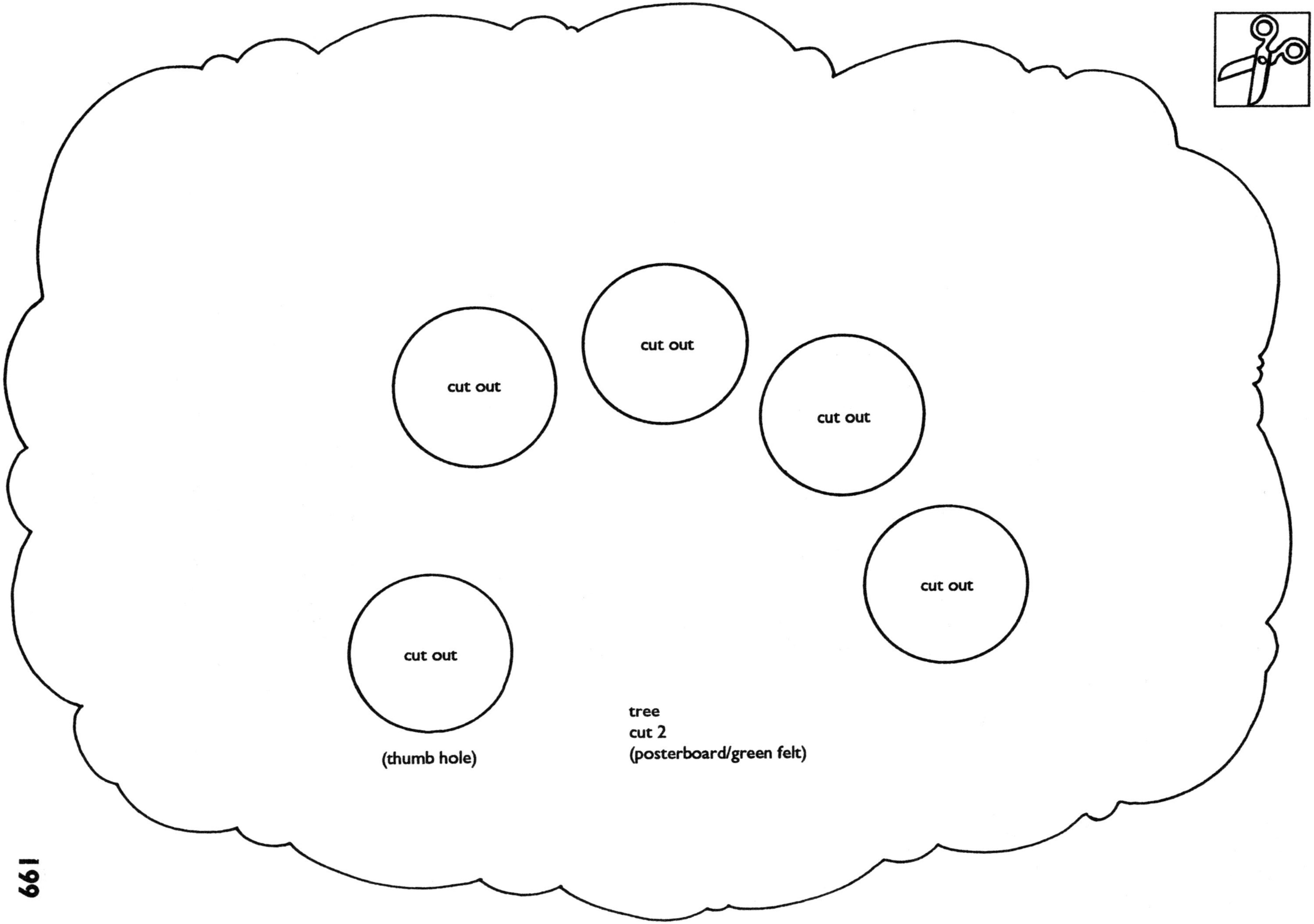

TWO BROWN MICE

MATERIALS

- patterns (page 202)
- felt
  brown (8" x 8") (20.3 cm x 20.3 cm)
  pink scrap
- 2 pink pom-poms (5 mm)
- 4 wiggly eyes (8 mm)
- black carpet thread and needle
- fiberfill
- pins

Mice

1. Cut four mouse bodies (page 202) from brown felt.
2. Pin each pair of body pieces together and set aside.
3. Cut eight feet (page 202) and four outer ears (page 202) from brown felt. Cut eight footpads (page 202) and four inner ears (page 202) from pink felt.
4. Glue a foot pad to each foot and glue an inner ear to each outer ear.
5. Place two ears together, pink sides out, and insert them between the body pieces of each mouse where indicated by the dotted lines. Pin the ears in place.
6. Put each pair of feet together, pink sides in, and insert two pairs of feet between the body pieces of each mouse where indicated by the dotted lines. Pin the feet in place.

7. Sew around the mouse bodies, being sure to catch the ears and feet in the stitches. Leave the straight end of each mouse open.
8. Turn the mice inside out.
9. Glue a pink pom-pom to the tip of each mouse nose.
10. Sew three 1 1/2-inch (3.9 cm) strands of black carpet thread through both sides of each mouse face just behind the nose.
11. Glue a wiggly eye to each side of both mouse heads.
12. Stuff each mouse lightly with fiberfill and adjust to fit your index fingers.

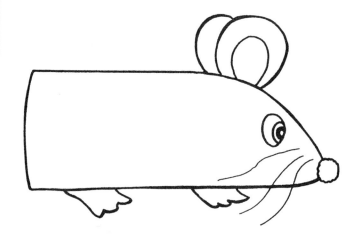

Two Brown Mice
(Tune: "Three Blind Mice")

Two brown mice
(Perch the mice on the front edge
of the box.)
I think they're nice.
I think they're nice.
They have pink ears and little
pink noses.
They run all around
On their little pink toes.

(Run the mice from side to side
along the box front.)
They don't wear shoes
And they don't wear clothes,
These two brown mice, two brown
mice.

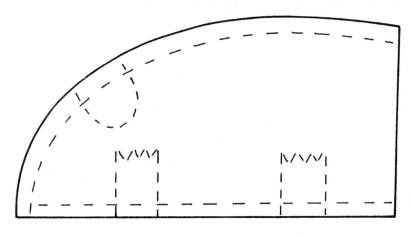

mouse body
cut 4
(brown felt)

foot
cut 8
(brown felt)

foot pad
cut 8
(pink felt)

inner ear
cut 4
(pink felt)

outer ear
cut 4
(brown felt)

PUPPETS, POEMS, & SONGS © 1993 Fearon Teacher Aids

TWO LITTLE BEAR CUBS

MATERIALS

- patterns (page 205)
- 8 paper plates (7") (17.7 cm)
- black felt scrap
- paint (brown and tan or beige)
- 4 wiggly eyes (25 mm)
- 2 foam-rubber cubes ($^1/_2$") (1.3 cm)
- black marker

Bear Cub Paper-Plate Puppets

1. Paint the bottoms of six paper plates brown and the bottoms of two paper plates tan or beige. Let the paint dry thoroughly.
2. Trace and cut two bear muzzles (page 205) and four inner ears (page 205) from the beige paper plates.
3. Glue a foam-rubber cube to the back of each muzzle. Then glue the muzzle, cube-side down, to the center bottom of a brown paper plate.
4. Cut four outer ears (page 205) from two other brown paper plates. Glue each inner ear to an outer ear.
5. Glue two wiggly eyes to each bear face above the muzzle.
6. Cut two noses (page 205) from black felt and glue each nose to a muzzle where indicated by the dotted lines.

7. Using a black marker, draw mouth lines on the muzzles below the nose.
8. Staple the ears to the face plates.
9. Position the remaining two brown plates to the backs of the face plates. Staple the plates together around the edges, leaving an opening at the bottom large enough to fit your hand through.

Two Little Bear Cubs

Two little bear cubs went out to play,
(Hold up the bear-cub puppets.)
Over the hill and far away.
(Raise and lower the puppets and
move them to one side.)
They rolled and tumbled in the grass
so sweet,
(Roll your hands over each other.)
They sniffed all around for some
honey to eat.

(Perform the appropriate actions.)
Then two little bear cubs heard
their Mama call.
(Cock the puppet heads as though
they are listening.)
So they ran back home
(Run the bears behind your back.)
And that is all.
(Shrug.)

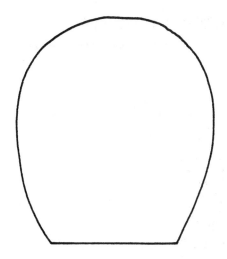

bear outer ear
cut 4
(brown plate)

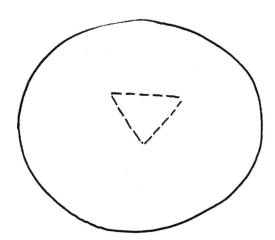

bear muzzle
cut 2
(beige plate)

bear nose
cut 2
(black felt)

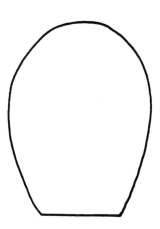

bear inner ear
cut 4
(beige plate)

BOOK CORNER

Barrett, Judi. *Animals Should Definitely Not Wear Clothing.* New York, NY: Atheneum, 1970.

Brown, Margaret Wise. *The Runaway Bunny.* New York, NY: Harper & Row, 1942.

Bunting, Eve. *The Mother's Day Mice.* New York, NY: Clarion, 1986.

Freeman, Don. *Corduroy.* New York, NY: Viking, 1968.

Galdone, Paul. *The Monkey and the Crocodile.* New York, NY: Clarion, 1969.

Galdone, Paul. *Three Little Kittens.* New York, NY: Clarion, 1986.

Galdone, Paul. *The Turtle and the Monkey.* New York, NY: Clarion, 1983.

Hill, Eric. *Spot's First Walk.* New York, NY: G.P. Putnam's Sons, 1982.

Hill, Eric. *Where's Spot?* New York, NY: G.P. Putnam's Sons, 1980.

Hoban, Tana. *Where Is It?* New York, NY: Windmill, 1974.

Kraus, Robert. *Whose Mouse Are You?* New York, NY: Macmillan, 1970.

Lionni, Leo. *Alexander and the Wind-Up Mouse.* New York, NY: Pantheon, 1969.

Livingston, Myra Cohn. *Cat Poems.* New York, NY: Holiday House, 1987.

Majewska, Joe and Maria. *A Friend for Oscar Mouse.* New York, NY: Dial, 1988.

Patterson, Dr. Francine. *Koko's Story.* New York, NY: Scholastic, 1987.

Payne, Emmy. *Katy No-Pocket.* Boston, MA: Houghton Mifflin, 1944.

Samuels, Barbara. *Duncan & Dolores.* New York, NY: Bradbury, 1986.

Tworkov, Jack. *The Camel Who Took a Walk.* New York, NY: E.P. Dutton, 1951.

GARDEN DELIGHTS

1. Make the box according to the instructions provided on page 16.
2. Cover the outside of the box with green or beige felt.

Garden Delights

WHAT DO YOU SUPPOSE?

MATERIALS

- pattern (page 209)
- interfacing (4" x 4") (10.2 cm x 10.2 cm)
- posterboard (4" x 4") (10.2 cm x 10.2 cm)
- black permanent marker
- crayons
- plastic straw
- book tape

Bee Stick Puppet

1. Using a black marker, trace a bee (page 209) onto interfacing.
2. Color and glue the bee to posterboard, then cut the bee out.
3. Tape a plastic drinking straw to the bee's back end.

PUPPETS, POEMS, & SONGS © 1993 Fearon Teacher Aids

POEM

What Do You Suppose?

What do you suppose?
(Fly the bee around.)
A bee sat on my nose.
(Land the bee on your nose and
look at it cross-eyed.)
And then what do you think?
He gave me a wink.
(Wink.)

And said, "I beg your pardon.
(Jerk the bee away from your
nose.)
I thought you were the garden."
(Fly the bee behind your back.)

bee
(interfacing)

PUPPETS, POEMS, & SONGS © 1993 Fearon Teacher Aids

Garden Delights

FIVE LITTLE PEAS

MATERIALS

- pattern (page 211)
- brown garden glove
- green felt (2" x 4") (5.0 cm x 10.2 cm)
- pom-poms
  5 green ($^1/_4$") (6 mm)
  5 green (1 $^1/_2$") (3.9 cm)
  10 wiggly eyes (5 mm)

Pea Pod Glove Puppet

1. Cut a pea pod (page 211) from green felt.
2. Glue five $^1/_4$-inch (6 mm) pom-poms, side by side, along the length of the pea pod.
3. Glue the pea pod, pom-pom side down, to the center back of the brown glove.
4. Glue a 1 $^1/_2$-inch (3.9 cm) green pom-pom to the fingernail side of each glove fingertip.
5. Glue two wiggly eyes to each pom-pom.

Five Little Peas

Five little peas
(Hold up your gloved fist.)
In a pea pod pressed.
One grew, two grew,
(Raise one finger and then the
second finger.)
So did all the rest.

(Raise the remaining fingers.)
They grew and they grew
And they did not stop.
Until one day
That pod went pop!
(Clap your hands.)

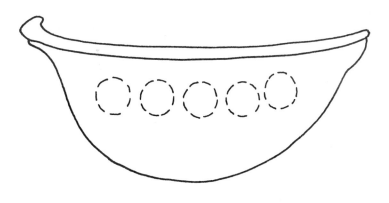

pea pod
(green felt)

Garden Delights

THIS IS THE WAY WE PLANT THE SEED
MATERIALS

- patterns (pages 215 and 216)
- felt
  beige (8" x 11") (20.3 cm x 28 cm)
  green scrap
  any color scrap
- yellow pom-pom (1") (2.5 cm)
- 2 wiggly eyes (3 mm)
- interfacing (6" x 6") (15.2 cm x 15.2 cm)
- posterboard (6" x 8") (15.2 cm x 20.3 cm)
- black permanent marker
- crayons
- paper cup (9 oz) (282 mL)
- 3 plastic straws
- book tape
- silver, blue, or iridescent tinsel

Flower Cup Puppet

1. Cut out the cup cover (page 215) and cover the paper cup with beige felt according to the instructions provided on page 25.
2. Carefully poke a hole the size of a pencil through the center bottom of the cup.
3. Cut one flower (page 216) from any color felt.
4. Glue the flower to posterboard and then cut the flower out.
5. Glue a 1-inch (2.5 cm) yellow pom-pom to the center of the flower.
6. Glue two wiggly eyes on the flower, then draw a smile on the flower.
7. Cut two leaves (page 216) from green felt and glue the leaves to the bottom of the flower.
8. Tape a plastic straw to the back of the flower. (Try using a silk flower instead of making one from felt. Mums, carnations, or other bushy flowers are very effective. Remember, the flower has to be small enough to be completely hidden inside the cup until the last verse of the song.)
9. Insert the straw down inside the cup through the hole in the bottom, so it can be pushed up from below to emerge from the top of the cup.

Rain Wand

1. Cut a narrow piece of book tape and put it aside temporarily by sticking one edge of the tape to the edge of a table.
2. Drape a small bundle (20 to 30 strands) of tinsel over your right index finger.

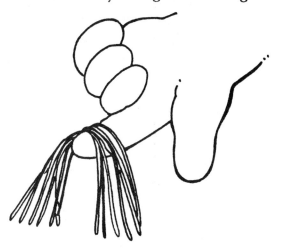

3. Grasp the bundle with your left thumb and index finger, just below the right index finger. Pull the resulting loop off your right index finger.

4. Insert the tip of the straw into the loop of tinsel just far enough to grasp it, along with the looped clump of tinsel, between your left thumb and forefinger.

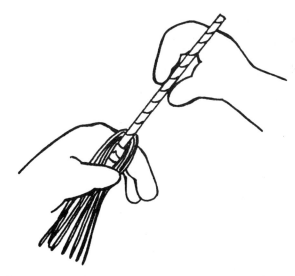

5. Tape the folded tinsel to the tip of the straw using the book tape you set aside earlier. Start the tape at the end and roll it tightly around the straw, being sure to catch all the tinsel.

6. The tinsel will hang down from one tip of the straw. Hold the straw by the other end and flutter downward to make rain.

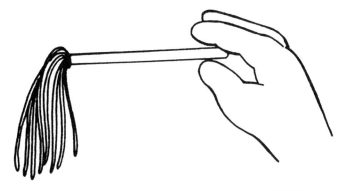

Garden Delights

Sun Stick Puppet

1. Using a black marker, trace a sun (page 216) onto interfacing.
2. Color and glue the sun to posterboard, then cut the sun out.
3. Tape a plastic straw to the back of the sun.

PUPPETS, POEMS, & SONGS © 1993 Fearon Teacher Aids

SONG

This Is the Way We Plant the Seed
(Tune: "Here We Go Round the Mulberry Bush")

This is the way we plant the seed
(Hold up the cup and place the imaginary seed inside.)
Plant the seed, plant the seed.
This is the way we plant the seed,
So early in the morning.
This is the way the rain will fall
(Shake the rain wand over the cup.)
Rain will fall, rain will fall.
This is the way the rain will fall,
So early in the morning.

This is the way the sun will shine,
(Hold the sun over the cup.)
Sun will shine, sun will shine.
This is the way the sun will shine,
So early in the morning.
This is the way the flower grows
(Slowly push the flower up out of the cup.)
Flower grows, flower grows.
This is the way the flower grows,
So early in the morning.

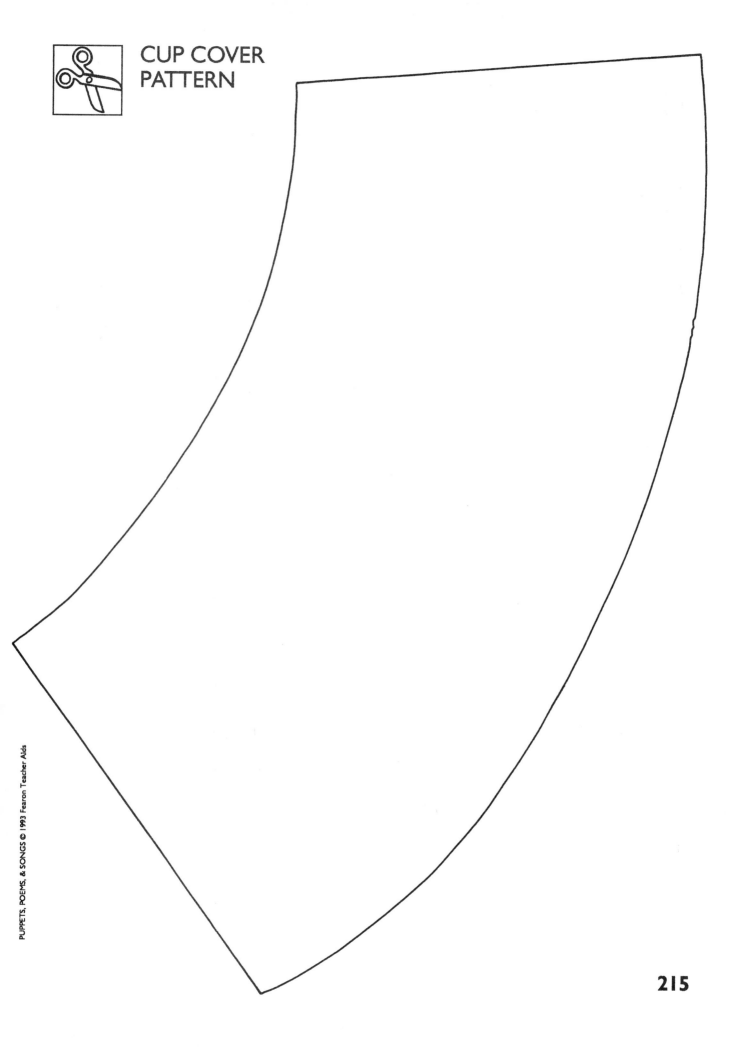

CUP COVER
PATTERN

sun
(interfacing)

flower
(felt)

leaf
cut 2
(green felt)

I TOOK A LITTLE CHERRY SEED

MATERIALS

- patterns (page 219)
- brown garden glove
- green felt (6" x 10") (15.2 cm x 25.4 cm)
- 10-15 red pom-poms ($^1/_2$") (1.3 cm)

Cherry Glove Puppet

1. Cut 20 to 30 cherry tree leaves (page 219) from green felt.
2. Glue two leaves to the palm side of the index fingertip of a brown garden glove. (This is an exception to the general rule for making glove puppets.)
3. Glue the remaining leaves at random on the palm side of the glove.
4. Glue $^1/_2$-inch (1.3 cm) red pom-poms among the leaves over the glove surface.

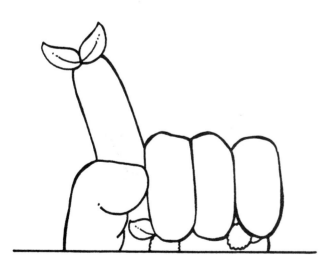

Garden Delights

POEM

PUPPETS, POEMS, & SONGS © 1993 Fearon Teacher Aids

I Took a Little Cherry Seed

I took a little cherry seed
And planted it, you see.
(Pretend to plant the cherry
seed in the box slot.)
And as the days and weeks
went by
There grew a tiny tree.
(Extend the tip of your gloved
index finger up out of the box.)
The tree grew taller day by day
And then what did I see?

(Slowly extend your arm upward
with your fist clenched to hide the
cherries.)
Bright red cherries everywhere!
(Open your hand to reveal the
cherries.)
I picked them, one, two, three.
(Pretend to pick the cherries.)
Mmmmmmmmmm!
(Rub your tummy and lick your
lips.)

218

cherry tree leaves
(green felt)

FIVE PINK TULIPS

MATERIALS

- patterns (page 221)
- garden glove
- interfacing (2" x 6") (5.0 cm x 15.2 cm)
- green felt (2" x 6") (5.0 cm x 15.2 cm)
- black permanent marker
- pink crayon

Tulip Glove Puppet

1. Using a black marker, trace five tulips (page 221) onto interfacing.
2. Color the tulips pink and then cut the tulips out.
3. Glue a tulip to the fingernail side of each glove fingertip, with the top of each tulip extending over the tips of the glove fingers.
4. Cut the stems and leaves (page 221) from green felt.
5. Glue stems and leaves to the glove fingers below each tulip.

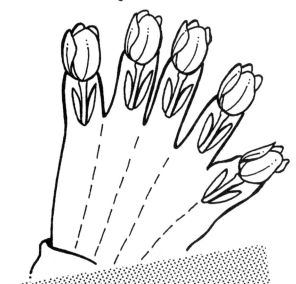

POEM

Five Pink Tulips

Five pink tulips growing by the door,
(Hold up your gloved hand.)
I picked one for Mother.
That left four.
(Lower the fingers one at a time as mentioned.)
Four pink tulips so beautiful to see.
I went and picked another one.
That left three.

Three pink tulips looking fresh and new.
So I picked another one.
That left two.
Two pink tulips glowing in the dawn.
I went and picked another one.
That left one.
One pink tulip lifting toward the sun.
Until I went and picked it.
That left none.

tulips
(interfacing)

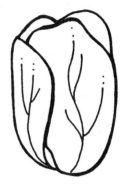

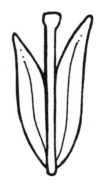

stems and leaves
(green felt)

MISTRESS MARY

MATERIALS

- patterns (page 224)
- interfacing (8" x 9") (20.3 cm x 22.9 cm)
- posterboard (8" x 9") (20.3 cm x 22.9 cm)
- black permanent marker
- crayons
- 6 wiggly eyes (3 mm)
- 4 plastic straws
- silver glitter
- small shells

Mary and Flower Stick Puppets

1. Using a black marker, trace Mary and the flowers (page 224) onto interfacing.
2. Color and glue the figures to posterboard, then cut the figures out.
3. Spread a thin layer of glue on the silver bells and sprinkle the bells with silver glitter. Shake off the excess glitter.
4. Glue small shells on the cockle shells.
5. Glue two wiggly eyes to each "pretty maid" in the row, then draw a smile on each flower.
6. Tape a plastic straw to the back of each stick puppet.

PUPPETS, POEMS, & SONGS © 1993 Fearon Teacher Aids

POEM

Mistress Mary

Mistress Mary, quite contrary
(Place each figure in the box slot
as mentioned.)
How does your garden grow?
With silver bells,
And cockle shells,
And pretty maids all in a row.

cockle shells
(interfacing)

Mistress Mary
(interfacing)

silver bells
(interfacing)

pretty maids all in a row
(interfacing)

PUPPETS, POEMS, & SONGS © 1993 Fearon Teacher Aids

FIVE LITTLE FLOWERS

MATERIALS

- patterns (page 228)
- garden glove
- brightly colored felt scraps
- 5 yellow pom-poms (1") (2.5 cm)
- 10 wiggly eyes (5 mm)
- interfacing (6" x 6") (15.2 cm x 15.2 cm)
- posterboard (6" x 6") (15.2 cm x 15.2 cm)
- black permanent marker
- crayons
- 2 plastic straws
- tinsel
- book tape
- decorating trim, such as yarn, sequins, or rickrack

Flower Glove Puppet

1. Cut five flowers (page 228) from various colors of felt.
2. Glue a flower to the fingernail side of each glove fingertip.
3. Glue a yellow pom-pom to the center of each flower.
4. Glue two wiggly eyes on each pom-pom.
5. Add other trim, such as yarn, sequins, or rickrack, to each flower.

Sun Stick Puppet

1. Using a black marker, trace a sun (page 228) onto interfacing.
2. Color and glue the sun to posterboard, then cut the sun out.
3. Tape a straw to the back of the sun.

Rain Wand

1. Cut a narrow piece of book tape and put it aside temporarily by sticking one edge of the tape to the edge of a table.
2. Drape a small bundle (20 to 30 strands) of tinsel over your right index finger.

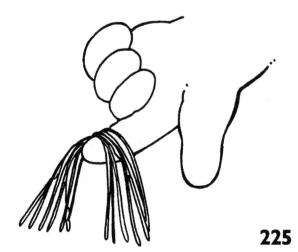

Garden Delights

3. Grasp the bundle with your left thumb and index finger, just below the right index finger. Pull the resulting loop off your right index finger.

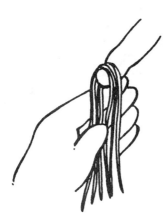

4. Insert the tip of the straw into the loop of tinsel just far enough to grasp it, along with the looped clump of tinsel, between your left thumb and forefinger.

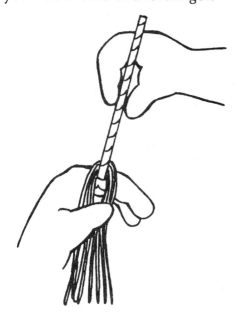

5. Tape the folded tinsel to the tip of the straw using the book tape you set aside earlier. Start the tape at the end and roll it tightly around the straw, being sure to catch all the tinsel.

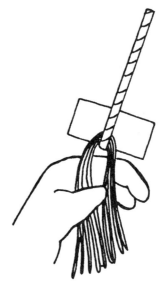

6. The tinsel will hang down from one tip of the straw. Hold the straw by the other end and flutter downward to make rain.

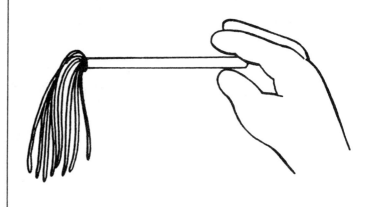

POEM

PUPPETS, POEMS, & SONGS © 1993 Fearon Teacher Aids

Five Little Flowers

Five little flowers
Are sleeping in their bed.
(Hold up your gloved fist with the
flowers hidden.)
A warm spring sun
(Hold up the sun.)
Is shining overhead.
Down come the raindrops

(Flutter the rain wand.)
Dancing to and fro.
And the five little flowers
Wake up and start to grow.
(Slowly straighten and spread
your fingers.)

flowers
(felt)

sun
(interfacing)

228

PUPPETS, POEMS & SONGS © 1993 Fearon Teacher Aids

BEG YOUR PARDON
MATERIALS
- patterns (page 231)
- pair of garden gloves
- felt
  pink (4" x 6") (10.2 cm x 15.2 cm)
  brown (4" x 4") (10.2 cm x 10.2 cm)
  brightly colored scraps
  white scraps
- pom-poms
  4 brown (1 ¹/₂") (3.9 cm)
  8 brown or contrasting color (¹/4")
  (6 mm)
  4 yellow (1") (2.5 cm)
- wiggly eyes
  8 (7 mm)
  8 (4 mm)
- decorating trim, such as yarn, sequins, or rickrack

Bunny Glove Puppet

1. Glue a 1 ¹/₂-inch (3.9 cm) brown pom-pom to the palm side of each glove fingertip on the left-handed glove. (This is an exception to the general rule for making glove puppets.) Glue nothing to the thumb.
2. Glue two ¹/4-inch (6 mm) pom-poms (either the same or a contrasting color as the larger pom-poms), side by side, just below the center line on each 1 ¹/₂-inch (3.9 cm) pom-pom. Glue the two smaller pom-poms to each other.
3. Cut four noses (page 231) from pink felt and four teeth (page 231) from white felt.
4. Glue each nose on top of the two small pom-poms, with the point coming down over the center seam between the two small pom-poms.

5. Glue the teeth to the center beneath the two small pom-poms.
6. Glue two wiggly eyes (7 mm) above each pair of small pom-poms.

7. Cut eight outer ears (page 231) from brown felt and eight inner ears (page 231) from pink felt.
8. Glue the inner ears to the outer ears. Place glue along the bottom edge of the assembled ears, then pinch the sides of the ears together to give the ears depth and shape and the stability to stand up straight.
9. Glue the ears to the top of the bunnies' heads.

Garden Delights

Flower Glove Puppet

1. Cut four flowers (page 231) from various colors of felt.
2. Glue a yellow pom-pom to the center of each flower.
3. Glue two wiggly eyes (4 mm) on each pom-pom.
4. Add other trim, such as yarn, sequins, or rickrack.
5. Glue a flower to the fingernail side of each fingertip on the right-handed glove. Again, glue nothing to the thumb.

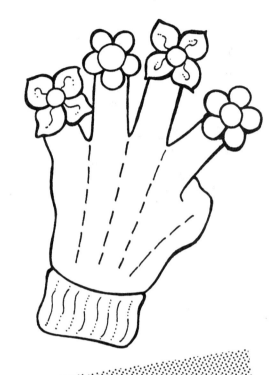

POEM

Beg Your Pardon

Some rabbits came over from Arden
(Hold up the left glove.)
And gobbled up most of my garden.
(Hold up the right glove.)
They feasted for hours
(Wiggle the bunnies against the flowers, gradually lowering your fingers so the flowers are out of sight.)

And ate all my flowers.
(Watch the bunnies hop away behind your back after the flowers disappear before saying the last line indignantly.)
And they never once said, "Beg your pardon."

flower
cut 2
(felt)

flower
cut 2
(felt)

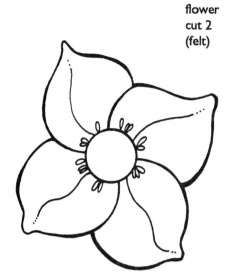

bunny outer ear
cut 8
(brown felt)

bunny inner ear
cut 8
(pink felt)

nose
cut 4
(pink felt)

teeth
cut 4
(white felt)

BOOK CORNER

Clark, Ann. *Tia Maria's Garden.* New York, NY: Viking, 1963.

Craft, Ruth. *Carrie Hepple's Garden.* New York, NY: Atheneum, 1979.

Ehlert, Lois. *Eating the Alphabet.* New York, NY: Harcourt Brace Jovanovich, 1989.

Fife, Dale H. *Rosa's Special Garden.* Niles, IL: Albert Whitman, 1985.

Galdone, Paul. *The Little Red Hen.* New York, NY: Clarion, 1973.

Gans, Roma. *Hummingbirds in the Garden.* New York, NY: Crowell, 1969.

Hurd, Thatcher. *The Pea Patch Jig.* New York, NY: Crown, 1986.

Krauss, Ruth. *The Carrot Seed.* New York, NY: Harper & Row, 1945.

LeTord, Bijou. *Rabbit Seeds.* New York, NY: Four Winds, 1984.

Petrie, Harris. *The Seed the Squirrel Dropped.* New York, NY: Prentice-Hall, 1976.

Potter, Beatrix. *The Tale of Peter Rabbit.* New York, NY: Warne, 1902.

Rockwell, Anne and Harlow. *How My Garden Grew.* New York, NY: Macmillan, 1982.

Steele, Mary Q. *Anna's Garden Songs.* New York, NY: Greenwillow Books, 1989.

Trimby, Elisa. *Mr. Plum's Paradise.* New York, NY: Lothrop, Lee & Shepard, 1976.

Tufts, Georgia. *Rabbit Garden.* New York, NY: Lothrop, Lee & Shepard, 1961.

Westcott, Nadine Bernard. *The Giant Vegetable Garden.* Boston, MA: Little, Brown, 1981.

Williams, Vera B. *Cherries and Cherry Pits.* New York, NY: Greenwillow Books, 1986.

NURSERY RHYMES

1. Make the box according to the instructions provided on page 16.
2. Cover the outside of the box with any color felt or self-adhesive paper with a small, subtle pattern.

LITTLE MISS MUFFET
MATERIALS

- patterns (page 235)
- garden glove
- felt scraps
  black
  skin-tone
- pom-poms
  1 yellow (1 1/2") (3.9 cm)
  1 black (2") (5.0 cm)
- 2 wiggly eyes (6 mm)
- calico ribbon (#9)
- black yarn
- miniature bowl
- miniature top hat

Miss Muffet

1. Glue a 1 1/2-inch (3.9 cm) yellow pom-pom to the index fingertip of the glove.
2. Make the girl's face, clothes, hands, and arms (see patterns on page 235) according to the instructions provided on page 19.
3. Glue a miniature bowl (or bowl cut from felt) to the center of Miss Muffet's dress and glue the hands to the underside of the bowl as though she's holding it.

Spider

1. Cut four 4 1/2-inch (11.4 cm) strands of black yarn.
2. Glue the centers of the yarn strands to the top of the glove thumb, arranged so they radiate outward from the center.
3. Cut eight circles (3/8 inch) (1 cm) for spider feet from black felt.
4. Glue one foot to the end of each yarn leg.
5. Glue a 2-inch (5.0 cm) black pom-pom on top of the leg centers.
6. Glue two wiggly eyes to the part of the pom-pom that faces the audience.
7. Add a miniature top hat or cut a hat from black felt.

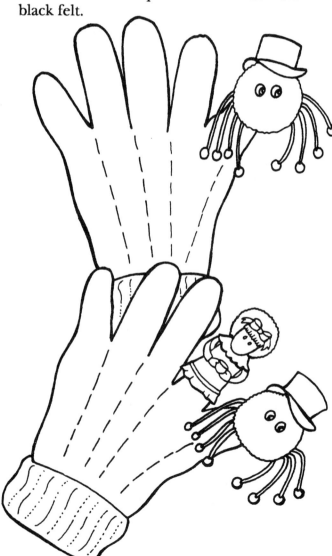

POEM

Little Miss Muffet

Little Miss Muffet
(Hold up your gloved index finger.)
Sat on her tuffet
Eating her curds and whey.
Along came a spider!
(Bring up your thumb.)
And sat down beside her!
And frightened Miss Muffet away!
(Lower Miss Muffet.)

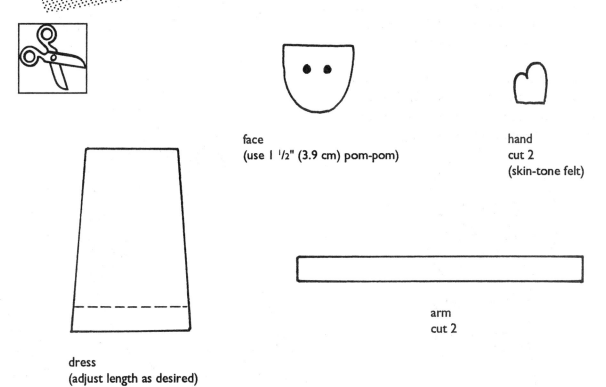

face
(use 1 1/2" (3.9 cm) pom-pom)

hand
cut 2
(skin-tone felt)

arm
cut 2

dress
(adjust length as desired)

JACK BE NIMBLE
MATERIALS

- patterns (page 237)
- interfacing (8" x 10") (20.3 cm x 25.4 cm)
- posterboard (8" x 10") (20.3 cm x 25.4 cm)
- black permanent marker
- crayons
- straw

Jack Finger Puppet and Candlestick Stick Puppet

1. Using a black marker, trace Jack and the candlestick (page 237) onto interfacing.
2. Color and glue the figures to posterboard, then cut the figures out.
3. Tape a straw to the back of the candlestick.

4. Insert your first two fingers through Jack's leg holes from behind to make legs.

Jack Be Nimble

(Insert the candlestick in the box slot before beginning the poem.)
Jack be nimble
(Run Jack from side to side along the front of the box.)
Jack be quick.
Jack jump over the candlestick.
(Jump Jack over the candlestick.)

Jump it lively,
(Jump Jack back and forth.)
Jump it quick.
Keep jumping over the candlestick.
(Continue jumping Jack over the candlestick a few more times.)

Jack
(interfacing)

candlestick
(interfacing)

cut out

cut out

cut out

Nursery Rhymes

OLD KING COLE

MATERIALS

- patterns (pages 241 and 242)
- garden glove
- felt
  skin-tone scrap
  red (4" x 8") (10.2 cm x 20.3 cm)
  purple (4" x 8") (10.2 cm x 20.3 cm)
  yellow scrap
  beige scrap
- pom-poms
  1 white (2") (5.0 cm)
  1 red (1") (2.5 cm)
  1 gold (1 1/2") (3.9 cm)
  1 beige (1 1/2") (3.9 cm)
  1 brown (1 1/2") (3.9 cm)
- gold or silver braid
- cotton ball
- 3 small feathers
- 3 flat wooden toothpicks
- interfacing scrap
- posterboard scrap
- black permanent marker
- crayons
- decorating trims, such as sequins or jewels

King Cole

1. Glue a 2-inch (5.0 cm) white pom-pom to the fingernail side of the glove index fingertip.
2. Make a man's face (see pattern on page 241) according to the instructions provided on page 21.
3. Glue a 1-inch (2.5 cm) red pom-pom to the top of Old King Cole's head for a crown.
4. Trim the red pom-pom with fancy gold or silver braid. Wrap the braid loosely around the bottom of the pom-pom.

5. Cut a cape (page 241) from red felt and a robe (page 241) from purple felt.
6. Glue the robe to the center of the cape where indicated by the dotted lines.
7. Fold the cape sides forward and down to meet in the center front of the robe. Glue the cape sides in place.
8. Trim the robe and cape with sequins or jewels.

Fiddlers

1. Glue a 1 1/2-inch (3.9 cm) gold pom-pom, a 1 1/2-inch (3.9 cm) beige pom-pom, and a 1 1/2-inch (3.9 cm) brown pom-pom to the fingernail side of the three remaining glove fingers. Glue nothing to the thumb.
2. Make three children's faces (see patterns on page 241) according to the instructions provided on pages 19–21. Then glue the faces to each of the three heads.

3. Cut three hats (page 242), three arms (page 242), and three tunics (page 242) from purple or red felt.

4. Cut six hands (page 242) from the same color felt as the faces.

5. Shape the fiddler's hats into cones, overlapping the ends slightly and gluing into place. The seam will be at the back of the hat.

6. Fold up the bottom edge of each hat about $1/4$ inch (6 mm) on each side and glue in place.

7. Glue a feather to one side of each hat.

8. Glue the hats to the fiddlers' heads.

9. Glue the arms to the top back of the tunics and glue the hands to the ends of the arms.

10. Glue the tunics to the glove fingers below the head pom-poms.

11. Paint three flat, wooden toothpicks brown.

12. Using a black marker, trace three fiddles (page 242) onto interfacing.

13. Color and glue the fiddles to posterboard, then cut the fiddles out.

14. Glue the fiddles to the fronts of the fiddlers, with the fat end of each fiddle underneath each fiddler's right chin

and the skinny ends coming down and away from their bodies toward the right at a slight angle.

15. Glue each right hand to the neck of the fiddle with the fingers curving up and over the front of the fiddle neck.

16. Arrange a flat toothpick across each fiddle like a bow and glue it into place. Glue each fiddler's left hand over the bottom end of the bow.

Bowl

1. Cut a bowl (page 241) from any color felt and cut the bowl contents pattern (page 241) from yellow felt.

2. Pull thin wisps from a cotton ball and glue them lightly in place above the bowl contents for steam. The fewer the wisps, the more real the steam will look.

239

Nursery Rhymes

Pipe

1. Cut a pipe (page 241) from beige felt.
2. Pull thin wisps from a cotton ball and glue them lightly in place above the pipe for smoke.
3. Glue both the pipe and bowl to the center back of the glove.

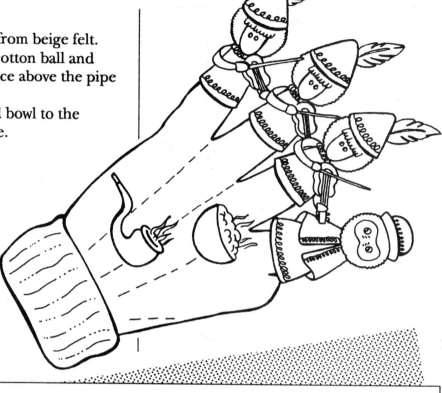

POEM

Old King Cole

Old King Cole
(Hold up your gloved index finger.)
Was a merry old soul,
A merry old soul was he.
He called for his pipe,
(Point to the pipe.)
He called for his bowl,
(Point to the bowl.)

And he called for his fiddlers three.
(Raise the remaining fingers.
Leave the thumb hidden.)
Old King Cole was a merry old soul,
A merry old soul was he.
Hooray for his pipe, hooray for his bowl,
And hooray for his fiddlers three.

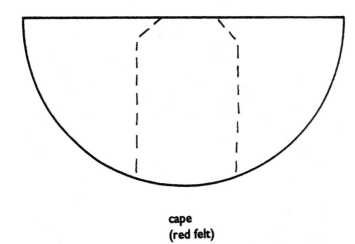

cape
(red felt)

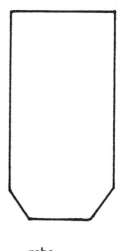

robe
(purple felt)

bowl
(felt)

bowl contents
(yellow felt)

pipe
(beige felt)

child's face
cut 3
(skin-tone felt)

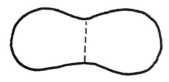

man's face
(skin-tone felt)

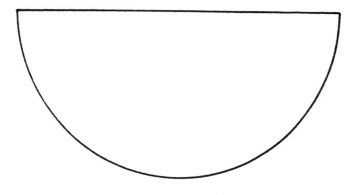

**fiddler's arm
cut 3
(purple or red felt)**

**fiddler's hat
cut 3
(purple or red felt)**

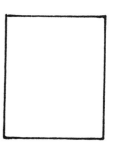

**tunic
cut 3
(purple or red felt)**

**fiddle
cut 3
(interfacing)**

**hand
cut 6
(skin-tone felt)**

PUPPETS, POEMS, & SONGS © 1993 Fearon Teacher Aids

MARY HAD A LITTLE LAMB

MATERIALS

- patterns (pages 246 and 247)
- garden glove
- felt scraps
  skin-tone
  white
  pink
  dark blue
- pom-poms
  1 yellow (1 ¹/₂") (3.9 cm)
  1 white (1") (2.5 cm)
  1 white (1 ¹/₂") (3.9 cm)
  1 white (2") (5.0 cm)
  1 black (1 ¹/₂") (3.9 cm)
  1 orange (1 ¹/₂") (3.9 cm)
- 2 half-rounds (3 mm)
- calico ribbon (#9)
- pink embroidery floss

Mary

1. Glue a 1 ¹/₂-inch (3.9 cm) yellow pom-pom to the fingernail side of the glove index fingertip.
2. Make a girl's face and clothes (see patterns on page 247) according to the instructions provided on **page 19**.

Lamb

1. Glue a 1 ¹/₂-inch (3.9 cm) white pom-pom to the thumb.
2. Glue a 1-inch (2.5 cm) white pom-pom to the center front of the larger pom-pom.
3. Cut two outer ears (page 246) from white felt and two inner ears (page 246) from pink felt.
4. Glue the inner ears to the outer ears. Glue the assembled ears to the sides of the head pom-pom.
5. Glue two half-rounds to the lamb's face, above the smaller nose pom-pom.
6. Glue curving threads of pink embroidery floss to the front of the small nose pom-pom. (Cut the threads longer than you need. Draw the curved lines on the pom-poms with glue and lay the embroidery threads into position. Cut off the excess thread after the glue is dry.)

Teacher

1. Glue a 2-inch (5.0 cm) white pom-pom on the second finger.
2. Make a man's or the woman's face, clothes, arms, and hands (see patterns on page 246) according to the instructions provided on pages 19–21.

3. Cut a book (page 246) from dark blue felt and pages (page 246) from white felt.
4. Glue the pages to one side of the book. Fold the book in half with the pages on the inside.
5. Glue the teacher's hands to the outside front and back covers of the book.

Children

1. Glue a 1 1/2-inch (3.9 cm) orange pom-pom to the ring finger and a 1 1/2-inch (3.9 cm) black pom-pom to the little finger.
2. Make two children's faces and clothes (see patterns on page 247) according to the instructions provided on pages 19–21. (Make one child a boy and one a girl, if you wish.)

POEM

PUPPETS, POEMS, & SONGS © 1993 Fearon Teacher Aids

Mary Had a Little Lamb

Mary had a little lamb,
(Hold up the gloved thumb and
index finger.)
Little lamb, little lamb.
Mary had a little lamb,
Its fleece was white as snow.
Everywhere that Mary went,
Mary went, Mary went,
Everywhere that Mary went,
The lamb was sure to go.
Followed her to school one day

(Raise the remaining fingers.)
School one day, school one day.
Followed her to school one day,
Which was against the rule.
Made the children laugh and play
(Wiggle the ring and little fingers.)
Laugh and play, laugh and play,
Made the children laugh and play
To see a lamb at school.

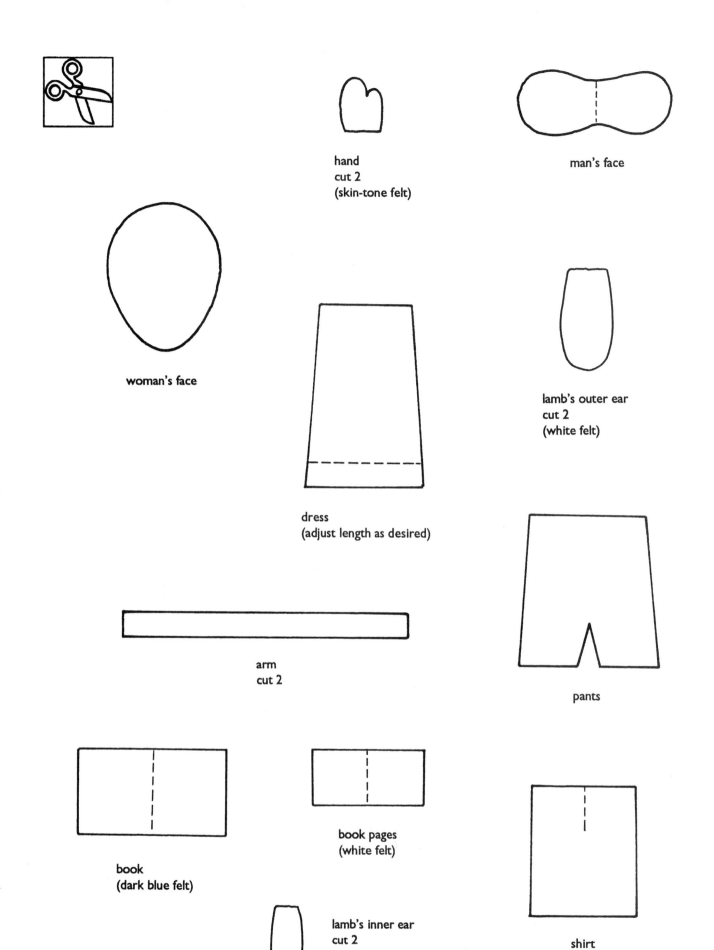

hand
cut 2
(skin-tone felt)

man's face

woman's face

dress
(adjust length as desired)

lamb's outer ear
cut 2
(white felt)

pants

arm
cut 2

book
(dark blue felt)

book pages
(white felt)

lamb's inner ear
cut 2
(pink felt)

shirt

246

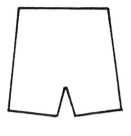

child's pants

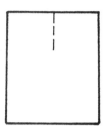

child's shirt

child's vest

child's face

THIS LITTLE PIGGIE

MATERIALS

- patterns (pages 250-252)
- 14 paper plates (7") (17.7 cm)
- felt
  white (7" x 8") (17.7 cm x 20.3 cm)
  black (3" x 6") (7.6 cm x 15.2 cm)
  green (4" x 7") (10. 2 cm x 17.7 cm)
  purple (4" x 8") (10.2 cm x 20.3 cm)
- posterboard (4" x 8") (10.2 cm x 20.3 cm)
- 10 wiggly eyes (20 mm)
- pink paint
- paintbrushes
- 5 foam-rubber cubes ($^1/_2$") (1.3 cm)
- false eyelashes
- 5 paint sticks
- book tape
- tin foil or blue iridescent or silver ribbon
- decorating trim, such as ribbon and silk flowers

Piggie Stick Puppets

1. Paint the bottoms of nine paper plates pink. Let the paint dry thoroughly.
2. Cut five noses (page 250), two eyelids (page 251), and five pairs of ears (page 250) from four of the pink plates.
3. Glue a foam-rubber cube to the back of each nose before gluing the noses to the centers of the five remaining pink plates.
4. Glue two wiggly eyes to each of the five pig faces.
5. On one of the pig's faces, glue the two eyelids over the wiggly eyes. Then add false eyelashes.
6. Glue the ears to the top sides of each head.

7. Cut a baker's hat (page 250) from white felt and glue the hat in place on one piggie.
8. Cut glasses (page 250) from black felt and glue the glasses to another piggie.
9. Cut a hair bow (page 252) from green felt or tie an actual ribbon in a bow and glue the bow to the piggie with the eyelids covering the eyes.
10. Cut one brimmed hat (page 251) from posterboard and one from purple felt. Glue the two hats together. Decorate the hat with trim, such as ribbon or silk flowers.
11. Glue the brimmed hat on another piggie.
12. Cut tears (page 250) from tin foil or iridescent blue or silver ribbon and glue the tears to the last piggie's cheeks.
13. Tape paint sticks to the eating surfaces of the five remaining unpainted paper plates.
14. Position each piggie-face plate to a back plate and staple the plates together around the edges.

PUPPETS, POEMS, & SONGS © 1993 Fearon Teacher Aids

POEM

This Little Piggie

This little piggie went to market
(Hold up the piggie with the bow.)
This little piggie stayed home.
(Hold up the piggie with the glasses.)
This little piggie had roast beef.
(Hold up the piggie with the baker's hat.)

This little piggie had none.
(Hold up the piggie with the brimmed hat.)
And this little piggie cried,
(Hold up the piggie with the tears.)
"Wee, wee, wee, wee!"
All the way home.

baker's hat
(white felt)

tears
(foil or ribbon)

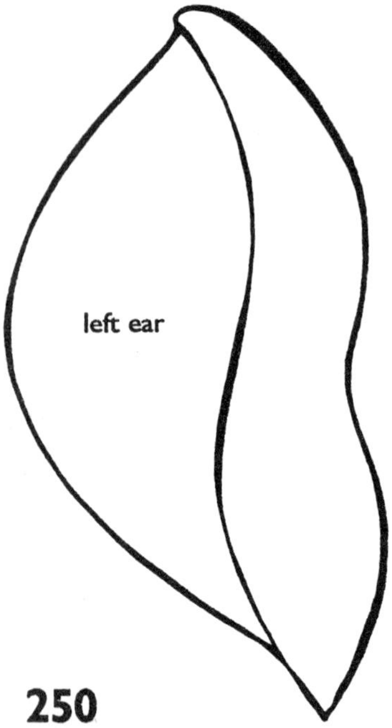

left ear

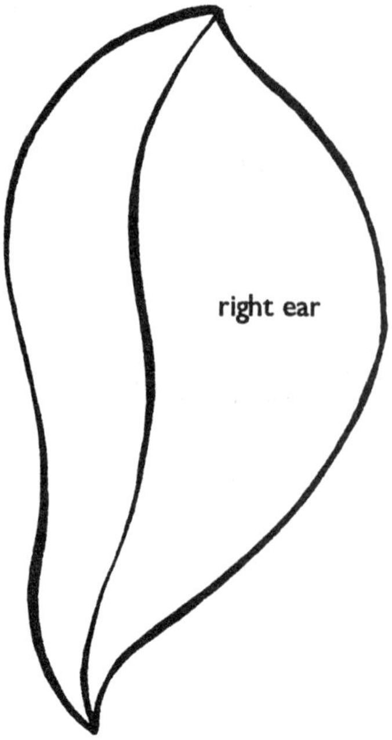

right ear

cut 5 pairs
(pink plate)

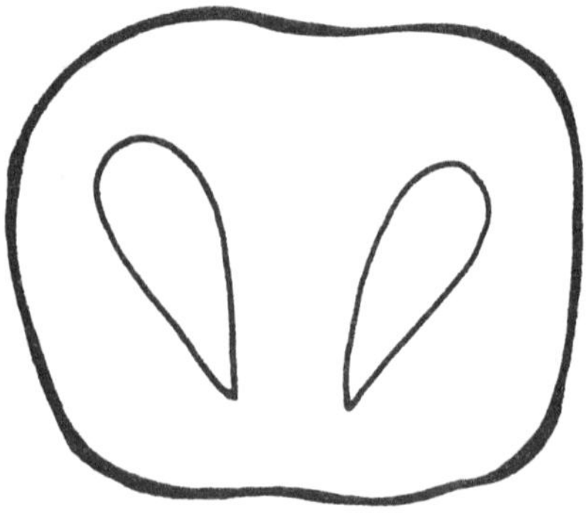

nose
cut 5
(pink plate)

250

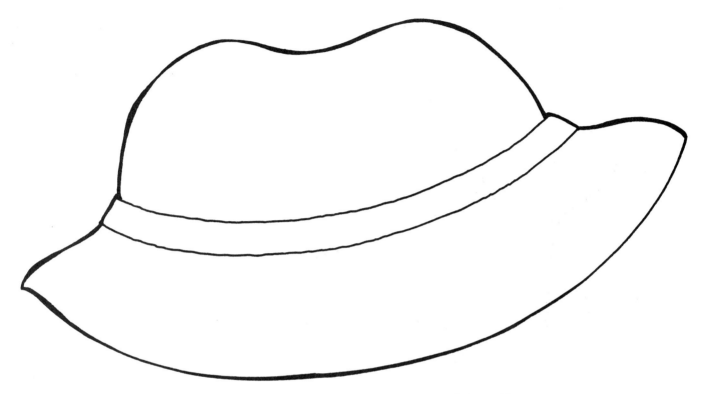

brimmed hat
cut 2
(posterboard/purple felt)

eyelid
cut 2
(pink plate)

hair bow
(green felt)

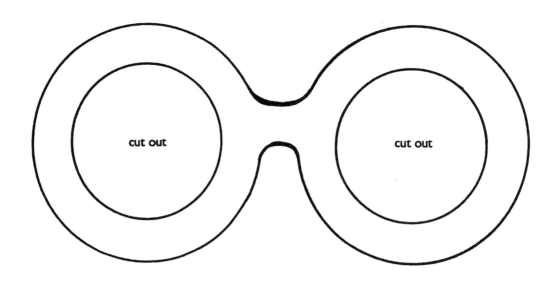

glasses
(black felt)

PUPPETS, POEMS, & SONGS © 1993 Fearon Teacher Aids

JACK-IN-THE-BOX

MATERIALS

- patterns (pages 255 and 256)
- felt
  red (5" x 5") (12.7 cm x 12.7 cm)
  skin-tone (3" x 3") (7.6 cm x 7.6 cm)
  purple (8" x 8") (20.3 cm x 20.3 cm)
  yellow (4" x 4") (10.2 cm x 10.2 cm)
  bright green (4" x 4") (10.2 cm x 10.2 cm)
- red pom-pom ($^1/_4$") (6 mm)
- 2 wiggly eyes (7 mm)
- posterboard
- red yarn
- decorating trim, such as sequins, fancy braids, and beads

Jack-in-the-Box

1. Cut a box (page 255) from red felt and a box from posterboard. Glue the two boxes together.
2. Trim the box with sequins or fancy braids.
3. Cut a head (page 255) from skin-tone felt and a head from posterboard. Glue the heads together.
4. Cut Jack's body (page 256) from purple felt, a collar (page 256) from yellow felt, and a hat (page 255) from bright green felt.
5. Glue the collar to the top of the body, being sure to match the straight edges.
6. Glue the head on top of the collar, matching the curved dotted line.
7. Glue the body to the box along the dotted lines.
8. Glue the hat to the top of the head.
9. Glue two eyes on the face.
10. Glue the curved piece of red yarn in place for the mouth.
11. Glue the red pom-pom on the face for the nose.
12. Trim the body and hat with the decorating trims.
13. Make a manipulator for the back of Jack's head according to the instructions provided on page 25.

PUPPETS, POEMS, & SONGS © 1993 Fearon Teacher Aids

POEM

Jack-in-the-Box

Jack-in-the-box
(Hold up the box with Jack hidden
behind it.)
So quiet and still
Will you come out?
"Yes, I will!"
(Pop Jack up.)

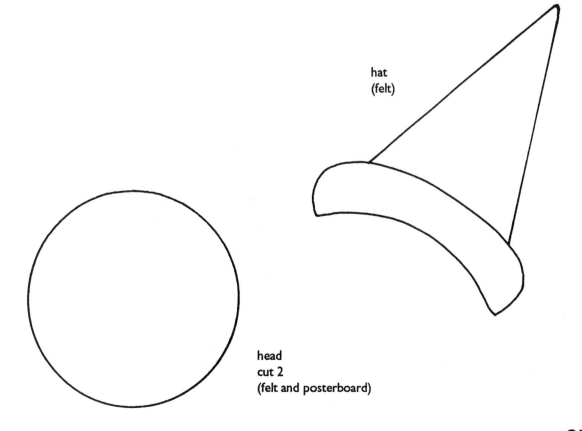

glue body here

box
cut 2
(felt and posterboard)

hat
(felt)

head
cut 2
(felt and posterboard)

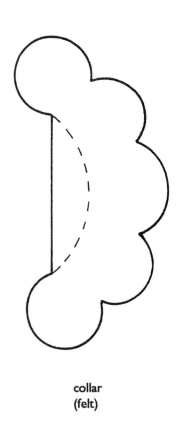

collar
(felt)

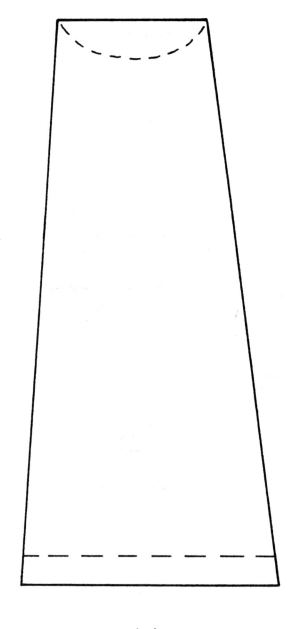

body
(felt)

256

HICKORY, DICKORY DOCK

MATERIALS

- patterns (page 259)
- paper plate (9") (22.9 cm)
- felt scraps
  pink
  white
- white plush fabric (5" x 6") (12.7 cm x 15.2 cm)
- posterboard (2" x 5") (5.0 cm x 12.7 cm)
- pink pom-pom (3 mm)
- 2 wiggly eyes (3 mm)
- black marker
- crayons
- brad fastener
- string
- black carpet thread and needle
- fiberfill
- hole punch
- pins

Clock Necklace

1. Using a black marker, write the clock numbers 1 to 12 around the backside of a paper plate.
2. Trace the clock minute hand (page 259) and the clock hour hand (page 259) on posterboard. Color the clock hands, then cut the hands out.
3. Attach the clock hands to the center of the clock face with a brad. (Punch a small hole in the paper plate and clock hands before inserting the brad to prevent the posterboard from ripping.)
4. Punch a small hole between the numbers 10 and 11 and between the numbers 1 and 2 on the clock.
5. Tie a string through the holes and make a loop long enough to hang the clock around your neck.
6. Add wiggly eyes and a face or fancy decorations to the clock, if desired.

Mouse Finger Puppet

1. Fold the white plush fabric in half with the right sides together.
2. Pin the mouse body pattern (page 259) on the fabric with the long straight edge along the fold. Cut out the mouse pattern.
3. Cut two outer ears (page 259) from white plush and two inner ears (page 259) from pink felt. Glue the pink inner ears to the plush side of the outer ears.
4. Place the two assembled ears together back-to-back, with the pink sides facing out. Insert the ears between the body pieces where indicated by the dotted lines. Pin the ears in place.
5. Sew the mouse along the seam line leaving the end open. Turn the material right-side out.
6. Glue a wiggly eye below the ear on each side of the mouse's head.
7. Glue a pink pom-pom to the point of the face for the nose.

8. Sew three strands of black carpet thread through the sides of the face, just behind the nose, for whiskers. Trim the whiskers to the desired length.
9. Cut a tail (page 259) from white felt.

10. Glue the tail to the top of the body along the seam, just inside the finger opening.
11. Stuff the puppet lightly with fiberfill and adjust to fit your finger.

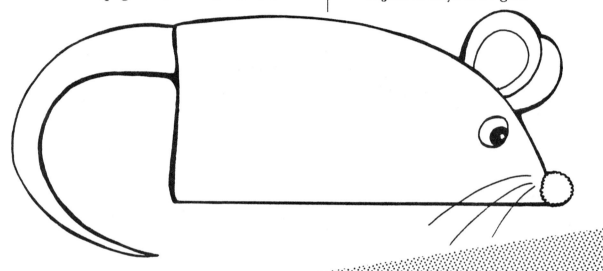

POEM

Hickory, Dickory Dock

Hickory, Dickory Dock
(Place the clock around your neck.)
A mouse ran up the clock.
(Run the mouse up the clock.)
The clock struck one

(Turn the clock hands to 1:00.)
The mouse ran down
(Run the mouse down the clock into the box.)
Hickory, Dickory Dock.

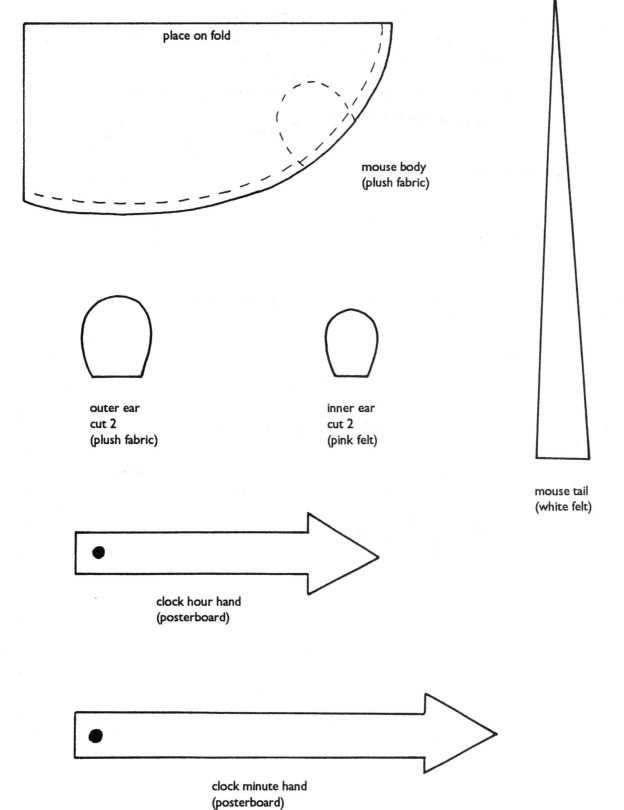

place on fold

mouse body
(plush fabric)

outer ear
cut 2
(plush fabric)

inner ear
cut 2
(pink felt)

mouse tail
(white felt)

clock hour hand
(posterboard)

clock minute hand
(posterboard)

BOOK CORNER

Alderson, Brian. *Cakes and Custard.* New York, NY: Morrow, 1975.

Brett, Jan. *Goldilocks and the Three Bears.* New York, NY: Dodd, Mead, 1987.

Brooke, Leslie. *Ring O'Roses.* New York, NY: Warner, 1922.

Cauley, Lorinda. *Three Little Kittens.* New York, NY: G.P. Putnam's Sons, 1982.

DeAngeli, Marguerite. *Book of Nursery and Mother Goose Rhymes.* New York, NY: Doubleday, 1954.

Galdone, Paul. *The Old Woman and Her Pig.* New York, NY: McGraw-Hill, 1960.

Hale, Sarah Josepha. *Mary Had a Little Lamb.* New York, NY: Holiday House, 1984.

Hawkins, Colin and Jacqui. *Old Mother Hubbard.* New York, NY: G.P. Putnam's Sons, 1985.

Langstaff, John. *Oh, A-Hunting We Will Go.* New York, NY: Atheneum, 1974.

Peppe, Rodney. *The House That Jack Built.* New York, NY: Delacorte, 1970.

Provensen, Alice and Martin. *The Mother Goose Book.* New York, NY: Random House, 1976.

Spier, Peter. *London Bridge Is Falling Down.* New York, NY: Doubleday, 1976.

Tripp, Wallace. *Granfa' Grig Had a Pig and Other Nursery Rhymes Without Reason.* Boston, MA: Little, Brown, 1976.

Tudor, Tasha. *Mother Goose.* New York, NY: Walck, 1944.

TASTY TREATS

1. Make the box according to the instructions provided on page 16.
2. Cover the outside of the box with bright pink felt.

Tasty Treats

HERE IS A BEAR

MATERIALS

- patterns (pages 264 and 265)
- felt scraps
  pink
  beige
  black
- brown plush fabric (10" x 24") (25.4 cm x 61 cm)
- interfacing (5" x 6") (12.7 cm x 15.2 cm)
- posterboard (5" x 6" (12.7 cm x 15.2 cm)
- black permanent marker
- plastic straw
- crayons
- book tape

Bear Hand Puppet

1. Cut two bears (page 264) from brown plush fabric, being careful to place the straight edge on the fabric fold.
2. Unfold both bears and place them together with the fuzzy sides out. Stitch or glue the bears together along the dotted lines.
3. Cut two inner ears (page 264), two paws (page 264), and a nose (page 264) from pink felt. Cut a face (page 264) from beige felt and two eyes (page 264) from black felt.

4. Glue the felt features in place on the bear.

Bee Stick Puppet

1. Using a black marker, trace a bee (page 265) onto interfacing.
2. Color and glue the bee to posterboard and then cut the bee out.
3. Tape a straw to the back of the bee.

POEM

PUPPETS, POEMS, & SONGS © 1993 Fearon Teacher Aids

Here Is a Bear

Here is a bear, the bear is fuzzy.
(Hold up the bear puppet and
stroke it with your free hand.)
Here is a bee, the bee is buzzy.
Bzzzz!
(Hold up the bee and flutter your
hand.)
The bee makes honey in a hollow
tree.
(Flutter the bee around in a circle.)

The bear likes honey to eat, you
see.
(Hold up the bear and have the
bear rub its paws together.)
Here comes the bear.
(Move the bear towards the bee
and touch the puppets together.)
Whooooops! There he goes!
(Run the bear behind your back.)

Here Is a Bear continued

The little bee stung him!
(Shake the bee.)
Right on the nose!
(Bring the bear back out, rubbing
its nose with its paws.)

Owwwwwww !
(Have the bear rub its eyes as
though crying.)

PUPPETS, POEMS, & SONGS © 1993 Fearon Teacher Aids

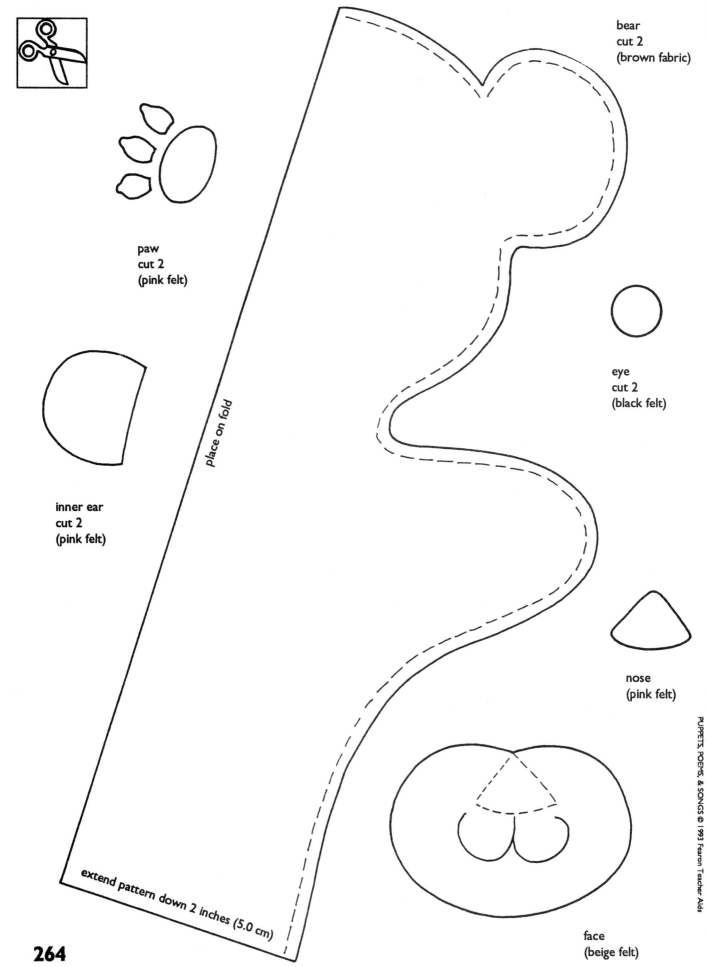

paw
cut 2
(pink felt)

bear
cut 2
(brown fabric)

eye
cut 2
(black felt)

place on fold

inner ear
cut 2
(pink felt)

nose
(pink felt)

extend pattern down 2 inches (5.0 cm)

face
(beige felt)

264

bee
(interfacing)

Tasty Treats

SIMPLE SIMON
MATERIALS

- patterns (page 268)
- interfacing (8" x 10") (20.3 cm x 25.4 cm)
- posterboard (8" x 10") (20.3 cm x 25.4 cm)
- black permanent marker
- crayons
- 2 plastic straws

Simple Simon and Pie-Man Stick Puppets

1. Using a black marker, trace the Simple Simon and the pie-man (page 268) onto interfacing.
2. Color and glue the figures to posterboard, then cut the figures out.
3. Tape a straw to the back of each figure.

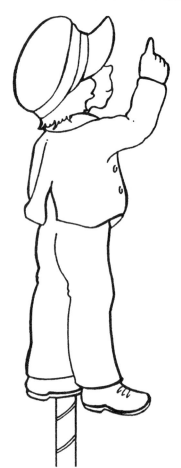

POEM

PUPPETS, POEMS, & SONGS © 1993 Fearon Teacher Aids

Simple Simon

Simple Simon met a pie-man
(Place each puppet in the box slot
as mentioned.)
Going to the fair.
Said Simple Simon to the pie-man,
"Let me taste your ware."
Said the pie-man to Simple Simon,
"Show me first your penny."
Said Simple Simon to the pie-man,
"Indeed, I have not any."
(Spread your hands and shrug.)

pie-man
(interfacing)

Simple Simon
(interfacing)

ONCE A LITTLE BUNNY

MATERIALS

- patterns (pages 271 and 272)
- 4 paper plates (7") (17.7 cm)
- pink felt scrap
- pink paint or pink permanent marker
- interfacing (6" x 8") (15.2 cm x 20.3 cm)
- posterboard (8" x 8") (20.3 cm x 20.3 cm)
- black permanent marker
- crayons
- lightweight monofilament fishing line
- foam-rubber cube ($1/2$") (1.3 cm)
- 2 wiggly eyes (30 mm)

Bunny Paper-Plate Puppet

1. Fold a paper plate in half.
2. Place the bunny ear pattern (page 271) on the plate, matching the curved edges. Trace along the pattern line. Cut on the line to make two ears.

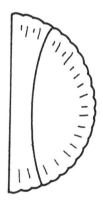

3. Paint the smooth part of the ears pink.
4. Cut a bunny face and teeth (page 271) from the second paper plate. Glue the teeth in place.
5. Cut nose (page 271) from pink felt and glue the nose to the center top of the bunny's face.

6. Glue fishing line to the bunny's cheeks for whiskers.

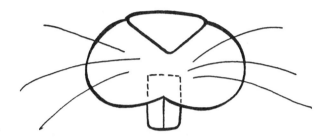

7. Glue a foam-rubber cube to the back of the face before gluing the face to the bottom (outside) of another paper plate.
8. Glue two wiggly eyes above the face.
9. Attach another plate to the back of the bunny-head plate. Then insert the ears between the two plates on top of the bunny head and staple the ears in place. The painted inner ears should be toward each other on the inside top of the head.
10. Staple the puppet around the edges, leaving enough space open along the bottom to insert your hand.

Tasty Treats

Lettuce

1. Using a black marker, trace the lettuce (page 272) onto interfacing.
2. Color and glue the lettuce to posterboard, then cut the lettuce out.
3. Fold a 2" x 4" (5.0 cm x 10.2 cm) posterboard strip in half and turn up each end 1 inch (2.5 cm). Pinch the strip together in the center and tape the ends to the back of the lettuce to make a handle.

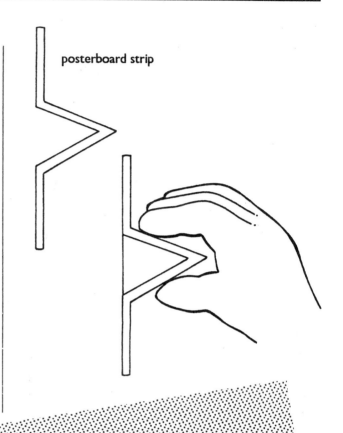

posterboard strip

POEM

Once a Little Bunny

Once a little bunny
(Hold up the bunny.)
Saw a lettuce head
(Hold up the lettuce.)
"Oh, boy, does that look tasty!"
The little bunny said.
So he went hopping, hopping, hopping
(Hop the bunny toward the lettuce head.)

Right over to his lunch.
And he made that lettuce disappear.
(Make nibbling motions with the bunny while gradually lowering the lettuce down into the box.)
Nibble, nibble, crunch!

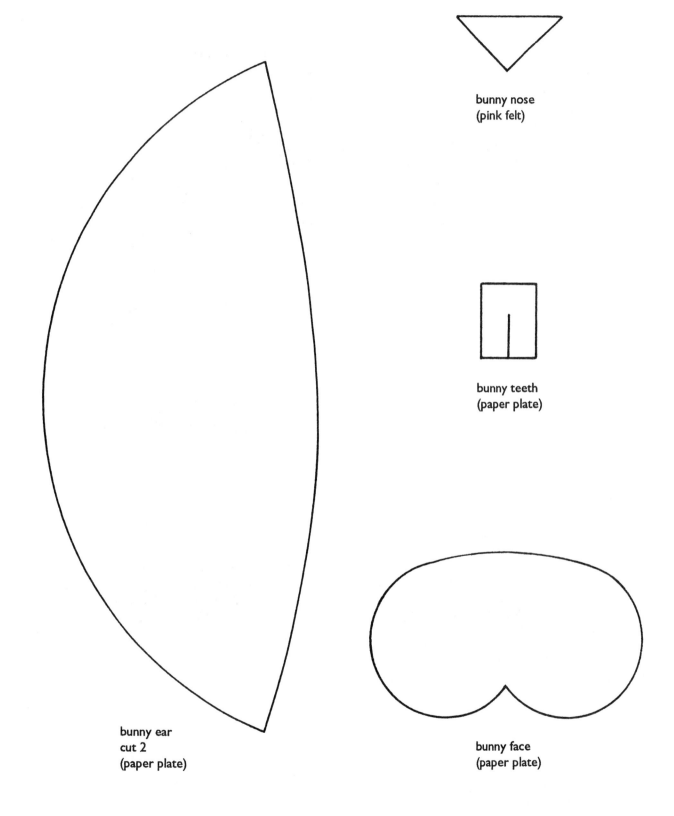

bunny nose
(pink felt)

bunny teeth
(paper plate)

bunny ear
cut 2
(paper plate)

bunny face
(paper plate)

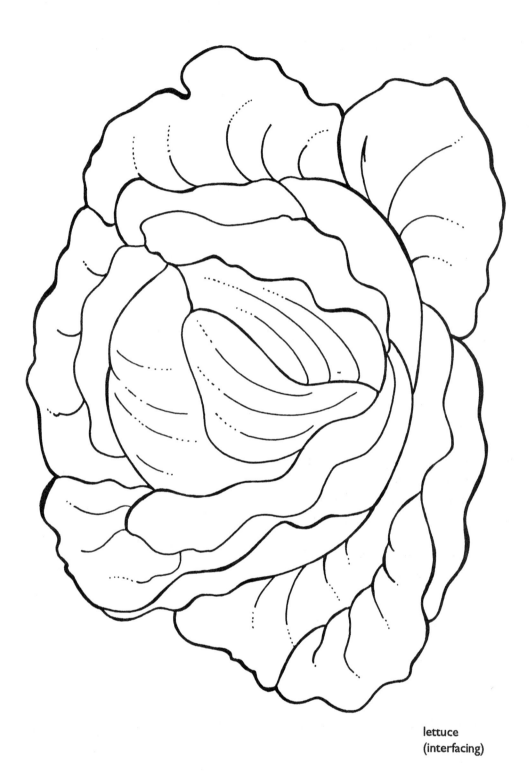

lettuce
(interfacing)

I ONCE SAW AN APPLE

MATERIALS

- patterns (page 276)
- 2 paper plates (9") (22.9 cm)
- felt scraps
  red
  green
- red paint
- apple seeds
- brown crayon
- felt, vinyl, or plush fabric (5" x 6") (12.7 cm x 15.2 cm)
- 2 wiggly eyes (15 mm)
- fiberfill
- needle and thread
- decorating trim, such as yarn, sequins, or pom-poms

Apple Paper-Plate Puppet

1. Paint the bottom of two paper plates red. Let the paint dry thoroughly.
2. Glue real apple seeds at random on the unpainted sides of the plates.
3. Cut two apple toppers (page 276) from green felt and two anchor strips (page 276) from red felt.
4. Cut a 2-inch (5.0 cm) diameter hole in the center of one paper plate.
5. On the red side of the plate without the hole, draw a small oval shape and color it brown for the soft, brown hole.

Worm

1. Cut two worms (page 276) from felt, vinyl, or plush fabric.
2. Stitch the worms together on the dotted line and turn the material inside out. Or, use hot glue around the dotted line.

3. Cut a mouth (page 276) from red felt and glue in place.
4. Glue a wiggly eye to each side of the worm's face.
5. Decorate with yarn hair, sequins, pom-poms, or feathers as desired.
6. Make tiny cuts, approximately ¼ inch (6 mm) deep, around the bottom end of the worm puppet.

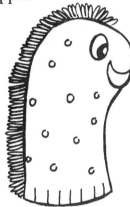

7. Push the worm through the 2-inch (5.0 cm) hole in the center of the red plate from back to front so the worm's head is on the unpainted side of the plate and the fringed bottom edge is just protruding onto the red side of the plate.
8. Fold the edges of the fringe over the edge of the hole and glue the tabs in place. This is the back side of the apple.

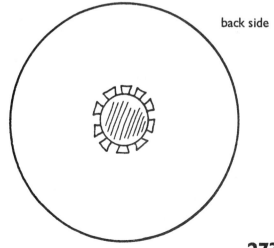

back side

9. Stuff the worm's head lightly with fiber-fill.
10. Staple the two plates together at the top edge with the red sides out. Be sure to put the plates together so that when the apple is opened, the worm is right-side up and looking at the audience.
11. Glue the apple toppers on matching spots on the front and back plates.

12. Place one red felt anchor strip along the top of the front plate. Glue each end to the plate, leaving enough room in the middle to insert your first two fingers.

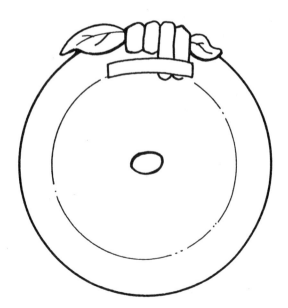

13. Glue the other anchor strip along the top of the back plate, leaving enough room for inserting your thumb.
14. To manipulate the puppet, slip the index and second fingers of your right hand underneath the front anchor strip on the top of the apple. Slip your thumb through the anchor strip on the back of the apple. Insert your left index finger into the worm puppet from behind the apple. At the appropriate point in the poem, open the apple and wiggle the worm.

POEM

PUPPETS, POEMS, & SONGS © 1993 Fearon Teacher Aids

I Once Saw an Apple

I once saw an apple
(Hold up the apple.)
All shiny and red.
It looked so delicious to me.
(Lick your lips.)
I opened my mouth
(Open your mouth wide.)
To take a big bite.
Uh-oh, what did I see?

(Jerk your head back.)
A wee little hole,
(Point to the hole.)
All soft and brown.
That apple had something inside!
I opened it up . . .
(Open the apple.)
And a worm looked at me!
(Wiggle the worm.)
With a grin on his face a mile wide!

mouth
(red felt)

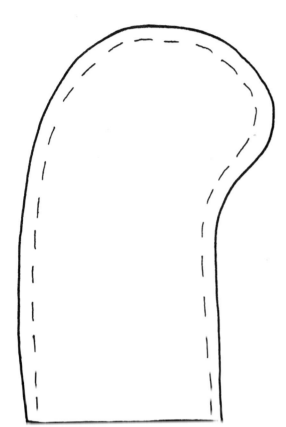

anchor strip
cut 2
(red felt)

worm
cut 2
(felt, vinyl, or plush fabric)

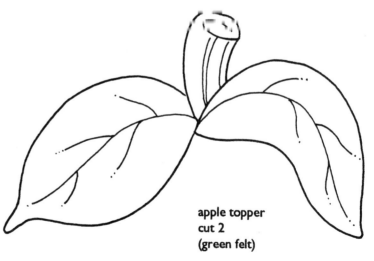

apple topper
cut 2
(green felt)

A FAT LITTLE FROG

MATERIALS

- patterns (page 280)
- 2 sturdy pink paper plates (9") (22.9 cm)
- felt
  red (4" x 4") (10.2 cm x 10.2 cm)
  green scrap
- green vinyl, satin, or shiny fabric
  (12" x 20") (30.5 cm x 50.8 cm)
- 2 green pom-poms (2") (5.0 cm)
- 2 wiggly eyes (40 mm)
- solid-color party blower (a curled-up
  paper tube that uncurls when you blow
  through the plastic mouthpiece)
- green paint
- book tape
- fiberfill

Frog Paper-Plate Puppet

1. Paint the bottom (outside) of one pink paper plate green. Let the paint dry thoroughly. (Sturdy party plates usually come in packages of eight or more and can be purchased at card or party supply stores.)
2. Fold the plate in half with the pink on the inside. This is the inside of the frog's mouth.
3. Place the mouthpiece of the party blower in the center of the plate along the fold and trace a circle around it. Cut out the circle and insert the mouthpiece through the hole. The blower material should be on the pink side of the frog's mouth and uncurl forward from the top when you blow through the mouthpiece. Cut off most of the mouthpiece so that only

half an inch protrudes out the back of the plate. Tape the mouthpiece in place on the green outside of the plate.
4. Cut a frog gullet (page 280) from red felt and glue to the center inside of the frog mouth. Position the gullet around the blower mouthpiece and along the plate fold where indicated by the dotted lines.

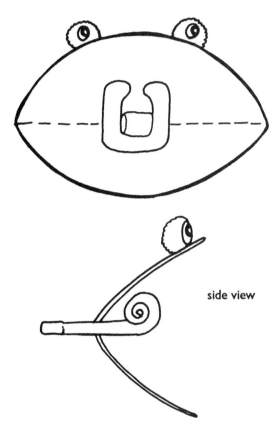

side view

5. Glue two green pom-poms to the top half of the folded plate, near the front, but not down on the rim.
6. Glue a wiggly eye to the front of each green pom-pom.
7. Cut two anchor strips (page 280) from green felt.

8. Glue the ends of one anchor strip to the top half of the frog's head (to one side of the protruding mouthpiece).

9. Glue the ends of the second anchor strip to the bottom half of the frog head (below the first anchor strip).

10. To manipulate the frog's head, put your index and second fingers under the top anchor strip and thumb under the bottom anchor strip. (With the anchor strips to one side, you can still hold and manipulate the puppet's mouth while blowing through the mouthpiece.)

14. Fold the neck tabs back and center the body on the lower jaw under the blower mouthpiece. Glue the wrong sides of both neck tabs to the underside of the lower jaw.

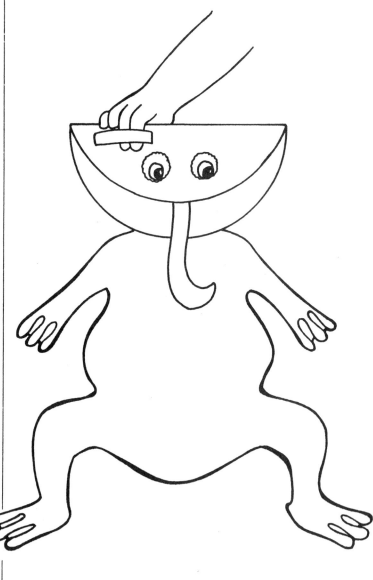

11. Cut two frog bodies (page 280) from green vinyl, satin, or any shiny fabric, placing the straight edge on the fabric fold.

12. Glue both pieces together around the edges with hot glue, leaving the top area around the neck tabs open.

13. Stuff the body cavity lightly with fiberfill.

PUPPETS, POEMS, & SONGS © 1993 Fearon Teacher Aids

POEM

A Fat Little Frog

A fat little frog came hop, hop, hop!
(Hop the frog up out of the box.)
He jumped on a log with a plop, plop, plop!
(Perch the frog on the box front.)
He sat very still and he rolled his eyes.
(Roll your eyes.)

Then out came his tongue
(On the word "out," blow through the blower so the frog's tongue comes shooting out.)
And he caught some flies!

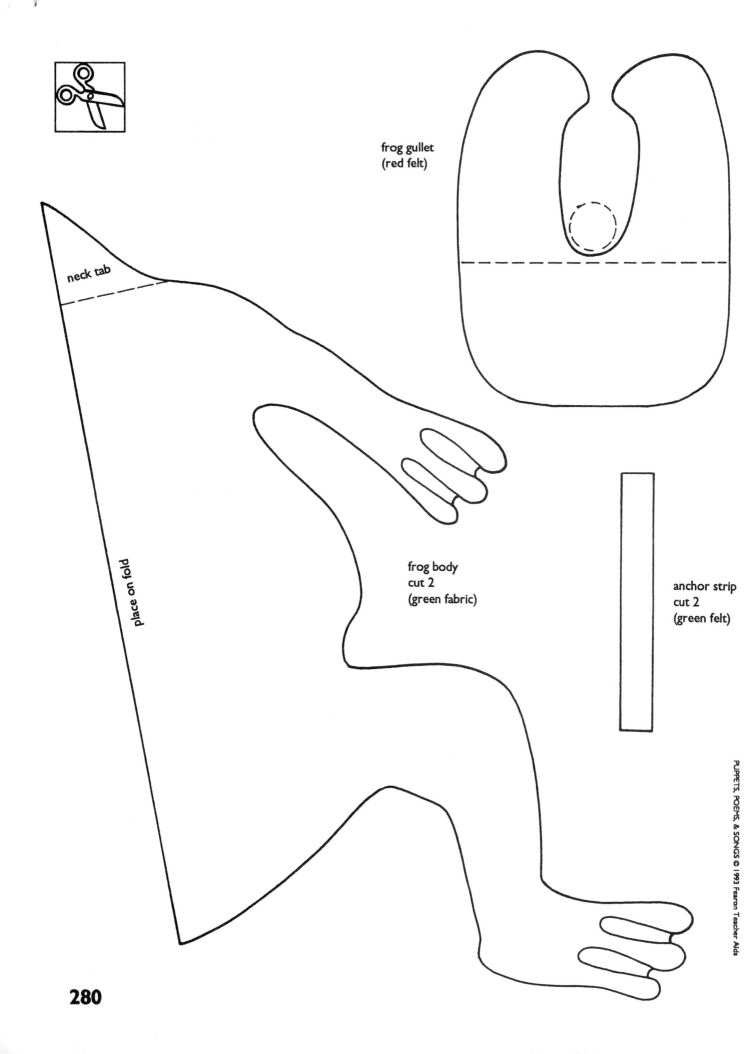

frog gullet
(red felt)

neck tab

place on fold

frog body
cut 2
(green fabric)

anchor strip
cut 2
(green felt)

280

I LOOKED UP IN AN APPLE TREE

MATERIALS

- patterns (page 283)
- garden glove
- felt
  red (4" x 6") (10.2 cm x 15.2 cm)
  brown scrap
  green scrap
- black permanent marker or black fabric paint
- 10 wiggly eyes (6 mm)

Apple Glove Puppet

1. Cut five apples (page 283) from red felt, five stems (page 283) from brown felt, and five or more leaves (page 283) from green felt.
2. Glue a stem behind the top of each apple and one or more leaves to each stem. (Instead of felt apples, you may want to use three-dimensional apples that are available, such as Christmas ornament apples, plastic apples, wooden apples, and refrigerator magnets.)
3. Draw a smile on each apple with black marker or fabric paint.
4. Glue two wiggly eyes to each apple.
5. Glue an apple to the fingernail side of each glove fingertip.

Tasty Treats

POEM

I Looked Up in an Apple Tree

I looked up in an apple tree
(Hold your gloved hand up high
revealing the fingers. Shade your
eyes and look up.)
And five red apples smiled down
at me.
I shook that tree as hard as I
could.
(Grab the wrist of the gloved
hand with your free hand and
shake.)

Down fell an apple!
(Lower one finger.)
Mmmmm, good.
(Pretend to eat the apple.)
(Keep your gloved hand up high
throughout the entire poem until
the last four lines. Repeat the
above actions in each verse.)

I Looked Up in an Apple Tree continued

I looked up in an apple tree
And four red apples smiled down
at me . . .

And three red apples smiled down
at me . . .

And two red apples smiled down
at me . . .

And one red apple smiled down at
me . . .

I looked up in an apple tree
And no red apples smiled down
at me.
My head was hurting,
(Place your free hand on your
forehead.)
My tummy was, too.
(Hold your tummy.)
So Mommy just said, "No more
apples for you!"
(Shake an admonishing finger.)

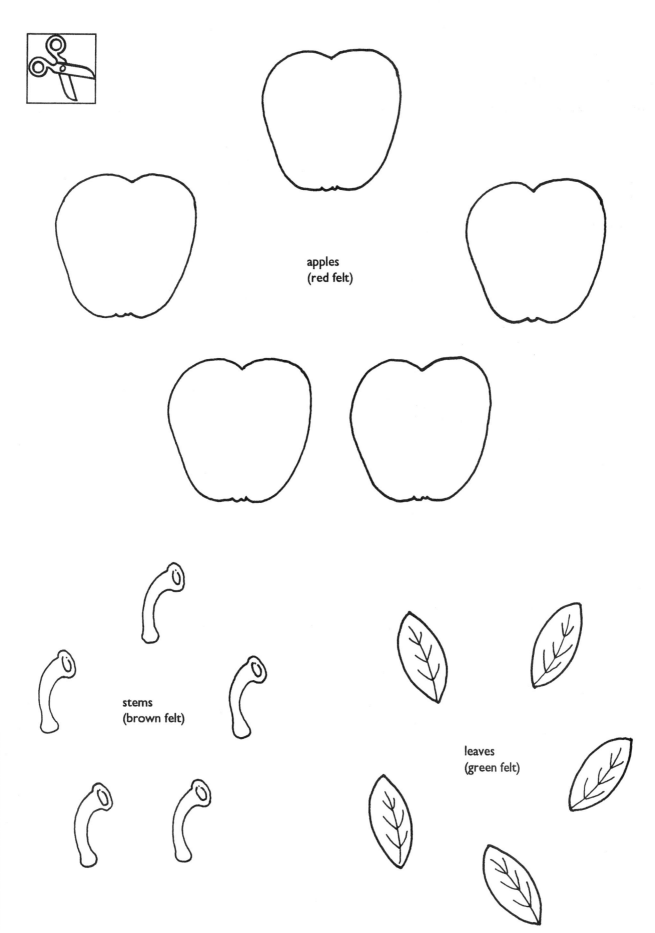

apples
(red felt)

stems
(brown felt)

leaves
(green felt)

STRAWBERRY, STRAWBERRY

MATERIALS

- patterns (page 287)
- 2 paper plates (7") (17.7 cm)
- felt
  red scrap
  green (4" x 5") (10.2 cm x 12.7 cm)
- felt, vinyl, or plush fabric (5" x 6") (12.7 cm x 15.2 cm)
- 2 wiggly eyes (15 mm)
- paint (red and yellow)
- fiberfill
- needle and thread
- paper towel

Strawberry Paper-Plate Puppet

1. Paint the bottoms of two paper plates red. Let the paint dry thoroughly.
2. Paint small yellow oval shapes at random on both red surfaces for seeds.
3. Paint the tops (eating surfaces) of the two plates with very watery red paint. Blot with a paper towel to give the inside of the strawberry a pale, blotchy appearance.
4. Cut two strawberry toppers (page 287) from green felt and two anchor strips (page 287) from red felt.
5. Cut a 2-inch (5.0 cm) diameter hole in the center of one paper plate.

Worm

1. Cut two worms (page 287) from felt, vinyl, or plush fabric.
2. Stitch on the dotted line and turn the material inside out. Or, use hot glue around the dotted line.

3. Cut a mouth (page 287) from red felt and glue in place.
4. Glue a wiggly eye to each side of the worm's face.
5. Decorate with yarn hair, sequins, pompoms, or feathers as desired.
6. Make tiny cuts, approximately $1/4$ inch (6 mm) deep, around the bottom end of the worm puppet.

7. Push the worm through the 2-inch (5.0 cm) hole in the center of the red plate from back to front so that the worm's head is on the pale side of the plate and the fringed bottom edge is just protruding onto the red side of the plate.
8. Fold the edges of the fringe over the edge of the hole and glue the tabs in place. This is the back side of the strawberry.

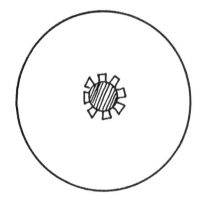

9. Stuff the worm's head lightly with fiberfill.
10. Staple the two plates together at the top edge with the red sides out. Be sure to

put the plates together so that when the strawberry is opened, the worm is right-side up and looking at the audience.

11. Glue a strawberry topper to the top of the front and back plates.

12. Place one red felt anchor strip along the top of the front plate. Glue each end to the plate, leaving enough room in the middle to insert your first two fingers.

13. Glue the other anchor strip along the top of the back plate, leaving enough room for inserting your thumb.

14. To manipulate the puppet, slip the index and second fingers of your right hand underneath the front anchor strip from the top of the strawberry. Slip your thumb through the anchor strip on the back of the strawberry. Insert your left index finger into the worm puppet from behind the strawberry. At the appropriate point in the poem, open the strawberry and wiggle the worm.

POEM

Strawberry, Strawberry

Strawberry, strawberry,
(Hold up the strawberry.)
Without a flaw, berry
You fill me with awe, berry.
I love you. A lot.
Strawberry, strawberry,
Looking so sweet, berry.

Maybe I'll eat you.
Then again,
(Open the plate to reveal the worm.)
Maybe not.

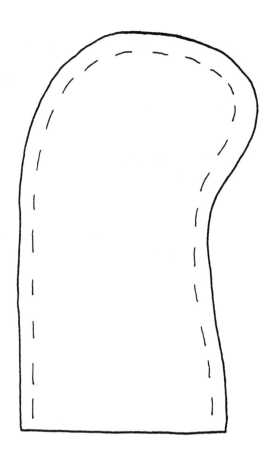

worm
cut 2
(felt, vinyl, or plush fabric)

mouth
(red felt)

anchor strip
cut 2
(red felt)

strawberry topper
cut 2
(green felt)

BOOK CORNER

Aliki. *Keep Your Mouth Closed, Dear*. New York, NY: Dial, 1966.

Berenstain, Stan and Jan. *The Bear's Picnic*. New York, NY: Random House, 1966.

Brown, Marcia. *Stone Soup*. New York, NY: Macmillan, 1947.

Demarest, Chris L. *No Peas for Nellie*. New York, NY: Macmillan, 1988.

DePaola, Tomie. *Strega Nona*. New York, NY: Prentice-Hall, 1975.

Gibbons, Gail. *The Seasons of Arnold's Apple Tree*. New York, NY: Harcourt Brace Jovanovich, 1984.

Ginsburg, Mirra. *Two Greedy Bears*. New York, NY: Macmillan, 1976.

Kahl, Virginia. *The Duchess Bakes a Cake*. New York, NY: Charles Scribner's Sons, 1955.

Kent, Jack. *The Fat Cat*. New York, NY: Parents' Magazine Press, 1971.

Lord, John Vernon. *The Giant Jam Sandwich*. Boston, MA: Houghton Mifflin, 1972.

Noble, Trinka Hakes. *The King's Tea*. New York, NY: Dial, 1979.

Schneider, Rex. *The Wide-Mouthed Frog*. Owing Mills, MD: Stemmer House, 1980.

Seuss, Dr. *Green Eggs and Ham*. New York, NY: Random House, 1960.

Still, James. *Jack and the Wonder Beans*. New York, NY: G.P. Putnam's Sons, 1977.

Van Woerkom, Dorothy. *The Queen Who Couldn't Bake Gingerbread*. New York, NY: Alfred Knopf, 1975.

Westcott, Nadine Bernard. *I Know an Old Lady Who Swallowed a Fly*. Boston, MA: Little, Brown, 1980.

Winter, Paula. *The Bear & the Fly*. New York, NY: Crown, 1976.